The Garden Tomb

ANDREW C. SKINNER

DESERET
BOOK

SALT LAKE CITY, UTAH

Library of Congress Cataloging-in-Publication Data

Skinner, Andrew C., 1951-
  The garden tomb / Andrew C. Skinner.
    p. cm.
  Includes bibliographical references (p.   ) and index.
  ISBN 1-57008-967-1 (hardbound : alk. paper)
  1. Jesus Christ—Mormon interpretations. 2. Jesus Christ—Burial.
3. Jesus Christ—Resurrection. 4. Church of Jesus Christ of Latter-day
Saints—Doctrines. I. Title.
  BX8643.J4S54 2005
  232.96'4—dc22

                                                                      2004022955

Printed in the United States of America   72076
Publishers Printing, Salt Lake City, UT

10   9   8   7   6   5   4   3   2   1

For family and friends
who have gone before

Contents

Introduction

My father was a powerful influence on me. I suppose a realist would say that I was overly protected, sheltered, perhaps even coddled, by my father. Maybe so. My father was an affectionate and very patient man. I know he loved my mother, my sister, and me. Perhaps his own formative years without a mother or father, as well as several years in the United States Marine Corps, made him a more sensitive soul, more nurturing with my sister and me. I came to love what he loved—God, Church, country, family, the underdog, and trout fishing. I idolized him. I knew I could trust him.

My father was a convert to The Church of Jesus Christ of Latter-day Saints, and he knew a great deal about correct principles and important doctrine. I remember significant, substantive discussions with him, just the two of us, about such things as the life of Jesus and what it meant to be a bearer of the priesthood. He said to me on more than one occasion that he would rather be a deacon in the Aaronic Priesthood than president of the United States. A priesthood holder, he told me, has more of the kind of power that really counts than do kings or presidents.

1

I liked that kind of inspiring encouragement. I never wanted to be president of the United States, but I always wanted to hold the priesthood. My father held the priesthood. The gospel of Jesus Christ was very important to him.

A significant childhood memory is of my father, sitting on the edge of his bed reading from the standard works every night. Quite probably that example is where I began to gain my own passionate interest in the scriptures. Of course, I now realize that in this, as well as in other matters, my father possessed flaws. He read the scriptures by himself. It would have been better had he read them with the family. But his unflagging, consistent practice of reading from the standard works before he went to bed (he retired early and arose early) left a powerful impression on me.

It came as a monumental blow when my father died suddenly right after Christmas the year I was fourteen. I was left nearly devastated. I did not know what to do. I could not understand why God would take him away. I was empty and lonely and cast adrift. All activities, all things, were empty and hollow. For a time I could not see how I would ever be happy again. Good men and women came to our home to comfort my mother, my sister, and me. They spoke of eternal family bonds and bore testimony of the certainty of the resurrection—that my father would live again. But I was not comforted. I was consumed with grief. I was not paying attention. I *could not* hear because I thought my world was gone.

Enter Jesus and his ancient disciples, the principal characters who are the subject of the story discussed in this present book. Jesus was a powerful influence on his disciples. Jesus was the foundation on which the disciples had built the last few years of their lives. He loved them, and they loved him.

But at 3 o'clock one Friday afternoon, Jesus died by

crucifixion. Though his death and burial inaugurated the final act in the grand drama that was the Atonement, his disciples did not know that they were witnessing the Atonement. They saw only cruelty, humiliation, suffering, and dissolution. Jesus did not look like the Messiah, let alone the Son of God, as he hung on the cross, died the ignominious death of a condemned criminal, and was buried in a tomb not his own.

Of course, the disciples did not comprehend the kind of messiah Jesus was, nor the meaning of his resurrection. When they laid Jesus to rest, they did not anticipate the glorious morning of his rising from death to immortality and eternal life. Death seemed like the end. "For as yet they knew not the scripture, that he must rise again from the dead" (John 20:9). Surely they felt a grief beyond belief—that is, if they felt anything at all through their numbness. In those first hours following Jesus' burial, death itself may well have looked like the ultimate victorious enemy.

Jesus' death left the disciples' world in a shambles. It left a hole in their lives just as the death of my father had left a hole in mine. It left them hurting and doubting. Even after Mary Magdalene and the other women had seen the risen Lord and reported it, most of the other disciples did not believe he had taken up his body again. It took several visits by the resurrected Savior to convince all of them. At first they *could not* hear, just as I could not hear, because they were consumed with grief and thought their world was gone, just as I had.

Many of us modern disciples, I think, have felt some sympathy for our counterparts in the early Church as we ourselves have tried to work through the death of a loved one. I think of what the ancients faced. For three intense years they followed their Master, the "prophet from Galilee," putting their trust in him as the Anointed One. They had given up much, in some cases everything, to embrace Jesus' superlative teachings, his exemplary life, and his promise of an eternal kingdom of glory beyond this fallen, mortal realm. Then their hopes were dashed on a Roman cross and in an unfinished, borrowed tomb. I can well imagine that for those uncertain, miserable hours of Friday evening through Sunday morning, the disciples felt devastated. They may well have thought that the enemy had won, once and for all.

The truth is that without the Savior's victory over death on that incomparable Sunday morning, death would have been the ultimate enemy. Death would have won. Without the resurrection there would have been no redemption. Resurrection is redemption! Even laying aside for a moment the miraculous and infinite sacrifice of Jesus for our sins and sufferings, resurrection itself redeems each one of us from the grasp of death and the ultimate subjugation to the devil. For without the resurrection, the spirits of all humankind *would* have become just like the devil. Listen to Nephi's sure witness:

> Wherefore, it must needs be an infinite atonement— save it should be an infinite atonement this corruption could not put on incorruption. Wherefore, the first judgment which came upon man must needs have remained to an endless duration. And if so, this flesh must have laid down to rot and to crumble to its mother earth, to rise no more.
>
> O the wisdom of God, his mercy and grace! For behold, if the flesh should rise no more our spirits must become subject to that angel who fell from before the

4

presence of the Eternal God, and became the devil, to rise no more.

And our spirits must have become like unto him, and we become devils, angels to a devil, to be shut out from the presence of our God, and to remain with the father of lies, in misery, like unto himself; yea, to that being who beguiled our first parents, who transformeth himself nigh unto an angel of light, and stirreth up the children of men unto secret combinations of murder and all manner of secret works of darkness. (2 Nephi 9:7–9)

I have great empathy for the Savior's ancient disciples as they witnessed the death and burial of their Master. For just those few hours before the resurrection, they were, of all human beings, most miserable (1 Corinthians 15:19). Without faith in, or any understanding of, the literal resurrection, they were without hope and spiritual stability, at least to some extent. Thankfully, they did not have to endure that trauma for very long. But even that short period was long enough.

Some may say that the early disciples brought it on themselves—that they should have had greater faith; that they should have paid more attention to their Master's promises and declarations about rising from the dead after three days; that they should have believed. But sometimes the death of someone we love so much can overwhelm us, even if only momentarily, and skew our perception of gospel concepts gained through years of instruction. Sometimes such an event can even cause some to question their beliefs and can be the ultimate test of faith. Certainly it causes many of us to reflect on our most cherished and deeply held convictions. As I reflect on my own experience with the death of my father, I now marvel at the strength of the ancient disciples. When I consider what they had to contend with and the brutality they witnessed, I frankly appreciate their endurance all the more.

Ultimately, the disciples were able to emerge from their darkness and misery into the brilliant light of truth. They came to *know* that Jesus was who he said he was. He had shed his blood and redeemed all humankind, just as he said he would. He went to the world of spirits and fulfilled Isaiah's prophecy of preaching deliverance to the captives, opening the doors of the prison, and ransoming the prisoners so that they could go free, just as he said he would. He reentered his sealed tomb, took up his physical body again, and appeared to many who thought their world and their hope had vanished forever, just as he said he would. Truly, he healed the brokenhearted, just as he said he would. He ascended to heaven to watch over his Church and reveal his will as well as himself to mortals on this earth until the time of his glorious second coming.

This, then, is the story that is told in the present volume. *The Garden Tomb* recounts the singular and sacred events that transformed the place of ultimate sadness into the place of ultimate triumph. It is the last in a three-volume series describing our Lord's infinite atonement, which began in the garden of Gethsemane, continued at Golgotha, and culminated in the Garden Tomb with the wondrous resurrection. Truly, the atonement of Jesus Christ, which of course includes his resurrection, is the single most powerful and important event that ever has occurred or ever will occur in time or all eternity. From Creation's dawn through all the ages of a never-ending eternity, nothing will equal in significance the sacred events that transpired from Thursday through Sunday of the most pivotal week in the history of our universe.

Having said that, I return briefly to the days of my own misery. Gradually, my family, my friends, and my Scoutmaster helped me out of my black hole. They would not leave me alone (no insignificant modeling of the Savior's message and example in this case). They engulfed me in affection and activity. But, as much as anything, I really believe the Atonement operated on my behalf in those days. The Spirit of the Lord lifted the fog, so to speak, and the Savior lifted my suffering. Now, many years later, the story discussed in the following pages—the story of the Garden Tomb and the first resurrection—means more to me than words can express. I am convinced of the truth of the Lord's promises of redemption and resurrection, and I cherish my associations with those, past and present, who have helped strengthen my conviction of those promises. It is my hope that those who read what follows will also have their own convictions of Christ's infinite mercy and saving power strengthened.

And after this Joseph of Arimathaea, being a disciple of Jesus, but secretly for fear of the Jews, besought Pilate that he might take away the body of Jesus: and Pilate gave him leave. He came therefore, and took the body of Jesus.

And there came also Nicodemus, which at the first came to Jesus by night, and brought a mixture of myrrh and aloes, about an hundred pound weight.

Then took they the body of Jesus, and wound it in linen clothes with the spices, as the manner of the Jews is to bury.

Now in the place where he was crucified there was a garden; and in the garden a new sepulchre, wherein was never man yet laid.

There laid they Jesus therefore because of the Jews' preparation day; for the sepulchre was nigh at hand.

JOHN 19:38–42

CHAPTER 1

A Garden Tomb

A t 3 o'clock in the afternoon of the final Friday of his life (the eve of Passover), Jesus of Nazareth breathed his last breath (Luke 23:46). He had been hanging, impaled, on a Roman cross for six hours, since 9 A.M., just outside Jerusalem's city wall (Mark 15:25; Luke 23:44). The place-name for the grisly death scene was *Golgotha* (Aramaic) or *Calvary* (Latin), meaning "a skull." Perhaps the name denoted topographical features (tradition identifies the site as an old stone quarry), or maybe it was a symbolic name representing death much the same way the image of a skull and crossbones connotes death. It has even been suggested that Golgotha may have been so named because executed criminals were buried nearby, and the skulls or bones from interred bodies became exposed, on rare occasions, due to the ravages of animals or the elements—though leaving any portion of a corpse unburied was contrary to Jewish law and would have been rectified immediately (Talmage, *Jesus the Christ*, 667).

Death by crucifixion was the most drawn out and painful of all forms of execution in the ancient world. Its horrors were known to all. It was looked upon by many as inhumane and revolting, and its practice was finally abolished by the Roman emperor Constantine the Great (d. 337). The welcome relief of death came to the victim of crucifixion as a result of complete exhaustion due to unrelenting, excruciating pain and congestive organ failure from the unnatural position of the body nailed to the cross (Talmage, *Jesus the Christ*, 655). The word *excruciating*, in fact, comes from the same root as does *crucifixion*.

Jesus suffered all of the pain and physical breakdown that every other victim of crucifixion suffered. But Jesus was no ordinary human being. He could not die until he *decided* to die and that required the spirit, power, life, and influence of his actual Father, our Heavenly Father—the Mighty Elohim—to be completely withdrawn from him so that he could determine the actual moment of his death. This total abandonment by his Father caused Jesus to cry out, in Aramaic, the opening words of Psalm 22: "Eli, Eli, lama sabachthani?—My God, my God, why hast thou forsaken me?" (Matthew 27:46) and then caused the "critical breakdown to occur in His bodily organs and tissues so that, when He willed that He should die, His spirit could readily depart into the spirit world" (Andrus, *God, Man, and the Universe*, 425).

MOURNING

All of the bystanders and onlookers who had gathered at Golgotha for the sole purpose of watching the spectacle of crucifixion that afternoon left the scene smiting their breasts (Luke 23:48), a sign of anguish or contrition (Luke 18:13). But those who were personal friends of Jesus, including the women who had followed him from Galilee, stood as witnesses of the Savior's crucifixion to the very end of the ordeal, first beholding events from a distance (Luke 23:49) and then near the cross (John 19:25–27).

To the faithful followers of Jesus who had been involved in one way or another in the wrenching and tragic drama of the previous twenty-four hours—and it was truly a tragic drama of unduplicated intensity—the Crucifixion must have seemed a heart-sickening end to all their messianic hopes. After all, "a dead Messiah was no Messiah at all," in the contemporary Jewish view of things (Walker, *Weekend That Changed the World*, 38). The atmosphere of gloom and doom at the site of the Crucifixion was undoubtedly magnified by the darkness that had gathered in the skies three hours earlier (Matthew 27:45).

The women who had ministered to Jesus so caringly, all of them nurturers and spiritual giants themselves, surely must have been wounded emotionally and spiritually beyond our comprehension. Though others may have been present, we know of four women who were at the cross along with John the Beloved: Jesus' mother; His mother's sister (Salome, the mother of the evangelist John and his brother James); Mary, the wife of Cleophas; and Mary Magdalene (Talmage, *Jesus the Christ*, 668). Death is challenging to deal with no matter what the circumstances. But when there has been great love, death brings great sorrow. This I know from personal experience and believe it was true for those closest to Jesus. In addition, their grief was intensified because they had not yet comprehended the glorious promise of resurrection: "For as yet they knew not the scripture, that he must rise again from the dead" (John 20:9). A modern revelation provides not only counsel but also insight into those natural, divinely understood and approved emotions that so easily come to the surface when we mourn. "Thou shalt live together in love, insomuch that thou shalt weep for the loss of them that die, and more especially for those that have not hope of a glorious resurrection" (D&C 42:45).

Sorrow, mourning, and tears have their place in God's plan. We humans are creations who are supposed to weep and mourn. In fact, we are commanded to love and to mourn! These feelings are what make us like our Creator. They are part of godhood. The realization that this is true seems to have greatly surprised the great seer Enoch when he witnessed the God of heaven crying. "And it came to pass that the God of heaven looked upon the residue of the people, and he wept; and Enoch bore record of it, saying: How is it that the heavens weep, and shed forth their tears as the rain upon the mountains? And Enoch said unto the Lord: How is it that thou canst weep, seeing thou art holy, and from all eternity to all eternity?" (Moses 7:28–29).

Enoch learned that God, the greatest of all, weeps and mourns. Apparently, he thought that because of God's infinite goodness, power, and knowledge, he was impervious to sorrow and emotion, or at least demonstrable emotion. It seems that he believed tears and outward displays of sorrow were not part of God's demeanor or his character: "And thou hast taken Zion to thine own bosom, from all thy creations, from all eternity to all eternity; and naught but peace, justice, and truth is the habitation of thy throne; and mercy shall go before thy face and have no end; how is it thou canst weep?" (Moses 7:31).

What Enoch learned, and what we learn, is that stoicism is for the birds—literally. Lesser creatures may not weep and mourn, but God surely does, and so must we.

I do not think it possible to overemphasize the sorrow Jesus' family and friends must have experienced. At that moment they did not possess the hope that only a knowledge of resurrection can bring. Even for those with a firm belief in the resurrection and the eternal nature of the soul, grief resulting from the death of one so dear can seem overpowering. How much more so is the case if that death is brought about by the brutality of others. As we contemplate what happened to Jesus, the unfairness and violence that engulfed him, and the sorrow that surely overwhelmed his mother and family members, no other circumstance can fully compare. Perhaps, however, there is something of a parallel in our own latter-day history—the martyrdom of the Prophet Joseph Smith. From the autobiography of Wandle Mace, we learn of reactions in Nauvoo to the death of Joseph Smith and his brother Hyrum. It takes little imagination to apply these same feelings to the family and friends of Jesus as they witnessed their beloved Master's crucifixion:

> Who can depict the scene? What pen describe the sorrow and mourning manifested by all? Strong men wept like children; women moaned as they gathered their little children around them and told them of the fearful crime that had taken place at Carthage, where the Governor had promised protection to those two innocent men, they had been left by him to be murdered.
>
> Who could describe the anguish of the families of those Martyrs? Their aged Mother who had already passed through so many trying scenes, she had seen her son dragged before the courts and discharged honorably because they could find no guilt attached to him, near fifty times—now he and her oldest son, two of earth's noblest sons, are shot down in cold blood by a mob, in the prime of life; their wives and innocent babes, left widowed and fatherless to face a relentless foe without the encouragement and assistance of those they dearly loved. ("Journal of Wandle Mace," 149)

To me, the words of Lucy Mack Smith, mother of the

Prophet Joseph Smith, when she described her feelings at the martyrdom of Joseph and Hyrum, convey more powerfully than most other writings the likely feelings of Mary and others at the foot of the cross.

On the morning of the twenty-fifth, Joseph and Hyrum were arrested for treason. . . .

I will not dwell upon the awful scene which succeeded. My heart is filled with grief and indignation, and my blood curdles in my veins whenever I speak of it.

My sons were thrown into jail, where they remained three days in company with Brothers Richards, Taylor and Markham. . . . Soon after this two hundred of those discharged in the morning rushed into Carthage, armed and painted black, red and yellow, and in ten minutes fled again, leaving my sons murdered and mangled corpses! . . .

Their bodies were attended home by only two persons. . . .

After the corpses were washed and dressed in their burial clothes, we were allowed to see them. I had for a long time braced every nerve, roused every energy of my soul and called upon God to strengthen me, but when I entered the room and saw my murdered sons extended both at once before my eyes and heard the sobs and groans of my family and the cries of "Father! Husband! Brothers!" from the lips of their wives, children, brothers and sisters, it was too much; I sank back, crying to the Lord in the agony of my soul, "My God, my God, why hast thou forsaken this family!" A voice replied, "I have taken them to myself, that they might have rest." Emma was carried back to her room almost in a state of insensibility. Her oldest son approached the corpse and dropped upon his knees, and laying his cheek against his father's, and kissing him, exclaimed, "Oh, my father! my father!" As for myself, I was swallowed up in the depths of my afflictions, and though my soul was filled with horror past imagination, yet I was dumb until I arose again to contemplate the spectacle before me. Oh! at that moment how my mind flew through every scene of sorrow and distress which we had passed, together, in which they had shown the innocence and sympathy which filled their guileless hearts. As I looked upon their peaceful, smiling countenances, I seemed almost to hear them say, "Mother, weep not for us, we have overcome the world by love; we carried to them the gospel, that their souls might be saved; they slew us for our testimony, and thus placed us beyond their power. (*History of Joseph Smith by His Mother*, 323–25)

Perhaps the great difference between Lucy Mack Smith and those at the cross of Jesus is precisely the difference John seems to emphasize: The early disciples did not comprehend the promise of a glorious resurrection (John 20:9). Their grief was not so easily assuaged. What was said by William Clayton of Joseph and Hyrum's mother surely must apply to Mary of Nazareth: "[She] is distracted with grief & it will be almost more than she can bear" (Allen, *Trials of Discipleship*, 142). It would be a wonderful thing indeed to learn someday that our Father in Heaven did give to Mary, the mother of his Divine Son, some measure of hope in the form of personal revelation, some little insight like that given to Lucy Mack Smith, so that Mary could know her Divine Son was at peace, that he was beyond the power of anyone to harm him anymore.

FULFILLING THE BURIAL CUSTOM

At some point Jesus' disciples must have realized that when the end finally came, if someone did not intervene, Jesus' body would simply be thrown into a common grave along with the bodies of other criminals crucified that day. A secret disciple of Jesus who had previously "feared" the Jews, perhaps because of his position in the Sanhedrin, did intercede, ultimately declaring himself to be a follower of Jesus by his bold action. This disciple was Joseph of Arimathea.

Joseph of Arimathea is a true hero. He is named in all four Gospels. He was a respected member of the great Sanhedrin, "an honourable counselor, which also waited for the kingdom of God" (Mark 15:43), "a rich man" (Matthew 27:57), and "a good man, and a just: [who] had not consented to the counsel and deed of them" (Luke 23:50–51). He bravely went to Pontius Pilate to acquire the body of Jesus and bury the lifeless remains of his Master in his own family tomb. If Jesus' body had been thrown into a common grave, it would have become the property of the Roman government. Joseph's action not only salved a bit of the anguish felt by Jesus' family and friends but also kept Jesus' physical remains a Jewish issue. "No doubt the religious authorities would not have been best pleased with this—not least because it meant that responsibility for Jesus' body was now once again within Jewish, rather than Roman, jurisdiction. But by this stage in the afternoon many of them were involved in the ceremonial 'waving of the first-fruits,' and so would only hear about Joseph's maneuver some hours later" (Walker, *Weekend That Changed the World*, 39).

The written testimony of John the apostle—the very same who was at Golgotha's cross with the women and who was commissioned to look after Jesus' mother—reports that Joseph was assisted by another member of the Sanhedrin, Nicodemus, in the burial detail (John 19:39–42). Their first task was to take down the body of Jesus from the cross. Although the Romans had no legal requirement that a victim's body must be removed from the cross (they often left corpses on their crosses to be scavenged by birds or wild animals), they allowed the Jews to follow their own law (Deuteronomy 21:23), which required "burial of a criminal the same day as his execution" (Maier, *In the Fullness of Time*, 176).

It is profoundly sobering to think of Joseph of Arimathea and Nicodemus, "two of Jerusalem's most distinguished leaders laboring in the darkening twilight to loosen the shattered remains of their Master from the horrible spikes" (Keller, *Rabboni*, 280). That had to have been a ghastly job, considering Jesus' physical appearance, but with love and care these loyal followers prepared his body for burial. Perhaps they shed many tears. Who could have performed such labor and not wept? I well remember grown men weeping on the day my father died and later as they helped with the burial arrangements. Their love and concern were moving. Their sensitive and thoughtful help was truly comforting. They showed my family that compassionate discipleship is not related to time, place, position, or convenience. They, like the disciples of old, reflected the image of the Master in their countenances.

Nicodemus didn't bring just a huge amount of embalming spices to prepare the corpse of Jesus—"about an hundred pound weight" (John 19:39)—but in fact a regal amount, representative of what was used in Israelite royal burials (2 Chronicles 16:14). Interestingly, Josephus mentioned huge quantities of spices in connection with the burial of King Herod the Great (*Wars*, 1.33.9; *Antiquities*, 17.8.3). This use of a large quantity of spices to prepare the Savior's body was another symbolic acknowledgment of his kingly status and the honorable burial he deserved.

Joseph and Nicodemus wrapped the Savior's body in layers of linen cloth, interspersed with Nicodemus's spices, myrrh, and aloes, according to the custom of the Jews (John 19:40). A smaller separate cloth, a *tallit*, or Jewish prayer shawl, according to tradition, was wrapped around the Savior's head. The corpse was then carried to the new, rock-hewn family tomb owned by Joseph. Some of the devoted women of the group, especially Mary Magdalene and the other Mary, observed the sepulchre and watched Jesus' body being laid to rest, but they did not enter the tomb. They intended to return to the sepulchre after they had observed the Sabbath day and then anoint the corpse with spices and ointments they had prepared (Luke 23:55–56; Mark 15:47; Matthew 27:61). But that was for another day. On Friday night everyone left the tomb. Because of the nearness of the Sabbath, Jesus' interment had to be accomplished hastily. At least his tomb was not too far away; neither was it unworthy of its occupant. Joseph was a rich man, and his new, unused sepulchre was located in a lovely spot—in a recognized garden, and the garden was "in the place where [Jesus] was crucified" (John 19:41).

John's Gospel mentions, almost in passing, "the burial custom of the Jews" (John 19:41). These customs are largely to be gleaned from passages of scripture:

> After death the body was washed, its eyes were closed and its mouth and other orifices were bound shut (Jn 11:44). A mixture of spices was applied to the body, perhaps as a preservation or perhaps to ward off the smell of decomposition for those who visited the tomb later (Jn 11:39; 19:39–40). It was then dressed in its own clothes

or placed in a linen shroud (Mt 27:59). Next, a procession, including musicians, family, and (if the family could afford it) professional mourners followed the corpse to the tomb (Mt 9:23). It was customary for mourners to continue to visit the tomb for 30 days, to reanoint the body (Mk 16:1) or to check to be sure the person had not been buried prematurely (Jn 11:31). (Matthews, *Manners and Customs of the Bible*, 239)

No procession is explicitly mentioned in scripture regarding the burial of Jesus, but surely one took place, even though it almost certainly omitted professional mourners and musicians because Jesus was regarded as a convicted criminal and because it was done in haste owing to the quickly approaching Sabbath. That the outcasts of society, including the poor, the strangers, social pariahs, and the criminally convicted, were buried in common unmarked, shallow graves (Luke 11:44) or in a "potter's field" (Matthew 27:1–10) makes us appreciate the service and sacrifice of Nicodemus and Joseph of Arimathea all the more. Because of them, the mortal body of the true King was allowed a clean and private resting place.

The Savior's Garden Tomb

No site mentioned in scripture has received more attention in Christendom than the Savior's Garden Tomb, even though its exact geographical location is not certain. Doctrinally, when we speak of the Savior's Garden Tomb, we come full circle to the inauguration of the plan of salvation on this earth, to another garden at the beginning of time, a garden called Eden. Major events of our Heavenly Father's plan of salvation, or great plan of happiness, have occurred in sacred gardens: the garden of

Eden, the garden of Gethsemane, and the garden of the Empty Tomb. The Creation, the Fall, and the Atonement thus become inextricably linked by gardens. The garden of the burial tomb, the site of Jesus' burial, resurrection, and completed atonement, is tied to the garden of Eden, the place where the Creation was completed and the Fall took place. Those gardens, in turn, are linked with the garden of Gethsemane, where Christ suffered for all the sin, sorrow, and pain resulting from the Fall and where he experienced his greatest suffering. Elder Bruce R. McConkie articulates this significant concept with apostolic power:

> As we read, ponder, and pray, there will come into our minds a view of the three gardens of God—the Garden of Eden, the Garden of Gethsemane, and the Garden of the Empty Tomb where Jesus appeared to Mary Magdalene.
>
> In Eden we will see all things created in a paradisiacal state—without death, without procreation, without probationary experiences.
>
> We will come to know that such a creation, now unknown to man, was the only way to provide for the Fall.
>
> We will then see Adam and Eve, the first man and the first woman, step down from their state of immortal and paradisiacal glory to become the first mortal flesh on earth.
>
> Mortality, including as it does procreation and death, will enter the world. And because of transgression a probationary estate of trial and testing will begin.
>
> Then in Gethsemane we will see the Son of God

ransom man from the temporal and spiritual death that came to us because of the Fall.

And finally, before an empty tomb, we will come to know that Christ our Lord has burst the bands of death and stands forever triumphant over the grave. ("Purifying Power of Gethsemane," 9–11).

For more than a century, two separate sites, each with its advocates, have been regarded as the possible location of Golgotha and the nearby Garden Tomb. One site, the earliest recognized location, is inside the Church of the Holy Sepulchre, west of the Temple Mount and within the present-day Old City walls. The other site is Gordon's Calvary, north of the Temple Mount and outside the present-day Old City walls.

Historians and archaeologists have generally favored the site inside the Church of the Holy Sepulchre. Traditions regarding its authenticity reach back to the second century after Christ when the Roman emperor Hadrian (A.D. 117–38) tried to remake Jerusalem into a thoroughly Roman town by obliterating the sites sacred to Jews and Christians. Over the place thought to have been Jesus' tomb, Hadrian erected a temple to Aphrodite (Venus).

In A.D. 325, during the council of Nicaea, Bishop Makarios of Jerusalem requested help from the emperor Constantine in restoring sacred sites. He immediately obtained permission to remove the Roman Temple of Aphrodite. The following year Constantine's mother, the intrepid seventy-nine- year-old Helena, made a pilgrimage to Jerusalem and directly contributed to the work of Christian restoration, which eventually resulted in the construction of the Church of the Holy Sepulchre.

The significance of the spot on which the Church of the

Holy Sepulchre was built, at least for Roman Catholic and Greek Orthodox Christians, lies in their belief that the church was constructed over both the Rock of Crucifixion (Golgotha) and the very tomb where Jesus was laid to rest before his resurrection. An eyewitness to the building excavations, Eusebius, the fourth-century historian and bishop of Caesarea, records: "At once the work was carried out, and, as layer after layer of the subsoil came into our view, the venerable and most holy memorial of the Savior's resurrection, beyond all our hopes, came into view" (Eusebius, *Life of Constantine*, 3.28, as quoted in Murphy-O'Connor, *Holy Land*, 50). That memorial was the empty tomb of Jesus.

In addition, according to a tradition dating from 351, Helena found fragments of the actual cross of crucifixion in a cave or cistern adjacent to the Rock of Crucifixion (also believed to be preserved inside the church) during her tour of Jerusalem in 326. The later provenance of this tradition makes it problematic, however.

At least two issues make the Church of the Holy Sepulchre unlikely as the site of Jesus' tomb. The first is a prohibition, extant in first-century Palestine, against placing burial sites to the west of Jerusalem. This prohibition is reflected in both the Talmud and the archaeological record. Reasons for its existence center on the requirements of ritual purity and the fact that prevailing winds in the Holy Land are from the west. As one scholar explained:

> Jews did not embalm dead bodies prior to burial; and corpses were left exposed in the tomb to desiccate, which could take over a year. Tombs to the west of the city presented two problems: (1) the scent of decomposing corpses would be carried over the city by breezes from

the west, and (2) Jews believed ritual impurity rising from interred corpses could be carried over the city by those breezes, causing the living inhabitants of the city to become "defiled" or unclean. (Chadwick, "Revisiting Golgotha and the Garden Tomb," 16)

Thus, Jerusalemites would have placed their tombs to the east, north, or south of the city but not to the west.

The prohibition against tombs to the west of Jerusalem also involved the Temple. From about 20 B.C. onward, Herod the Great and his successors supervised the expansion of the Temple and Temple Mount, making it the architectural jewel of the Mediterranean world. Modern scholars working in the Holy Land have shown that the beliefs and practices of the Pharisees were the basis for most Jewish practices, including those involving the Temple, during the Herodian period. The Pharisees predominated in the Sanhedrin during this time. Pharisaic tradition "would not have permitted tomb construction anywhere directly west of the expanded Temple Mount because wind passing over western tombs would also have passed over the sacred temple enclosure, thus defiling it and anyone in it" (Chadwick, "Revisiting Golgotha and the Garden Tomb," 17). Scholars thus conclude that since "burial customs in the first half of the first century C.E. [A.D.] preclude burials and their attendant impurities west (windward) of the Temple, then the crucifixion and burial of Jesus could not have taken place at the site of the Church of the Holy Sepulchre, which is almost exactly due west of the Holy of Holies" (Rousseau and Arav, *Jesus and His World*, 169).

The second issue bearing on the location of Golgotha and the Garden Tomb has to do with symbolism and typology. We know that all animal sacrifices in ancient Israel were a similitude and foreshadowing of the great and last sacrifice that would be made by Jesus Christ (Moses 5:4–8). The most important geographical symbolism associated with animal sacrifices and offerings of the Tabernacle and the Temple from Mosaic times onward required that the sacrifice of a lamb be made "on the side of the altar northward before the Lord" (Leviticus 1:11). In other words, the animal sacrifices—which constituted the most important elements of the various sanctuary offerings (burnt, peace, sin, etc.) and which symbolized the great and last sacrifice of the Son of God (Alma 34:13–14)—were slaughtered north of the altars of both the wilderness Tabernacle and the Jerusalem Temple. Therefore, wherever we look for the location of Golgotha and the nearby Garden Tomb, symbolic necessity dictates that we look north of the great altar of the Jerusalem Temple. This geographic symbolism is an important one of the many foreshadowings of the Lord's death and burial.

The other site that some believe to be the location of the Savior's death and resurrection, Gordon's Calvary, is often referred to simply as the Garden Tomb. It is an enclosed tomb and garden located near a skull-shaped hill overlooking the Old City of Jerusalem just north of Damascus Gate. It was identified only in 1883 as the crucifixion and burial site of Jesus by British General Charles ("Chinese") Gordon, just two years before he was killed at Khartoum. Some archaeologists and historians discount this site because there are no early historical traditions to authenticate it and because the tomb itself has been dated six centuries too early (from about the seventh century before Christ) by archaeologists. It must be noted, however, that latter-day prophets who have visited sites in the Holy Land have voiced some strong and impressive feelings about Gordon's

Calvary, or the Garden Tomb. Of this site President Harold B. Lee said in 1970:

> My wife and I were in the Holy Land. We have spent some glorious days visiting those places. . . .
>
> But a strange thing happened after we had gone to the garden tomb, and there we felt it was definitely the place. It was in the hill, it was a garden, and here was a tomb. . . . But the strange thing was that when we moved it seemed as though we had seen all this before. We had seen it before somewhere. ("Qualities of Leadership," 7)

Two years later President Lee reiterated his view of the Garden Tomb:

> We followed the way of the cross supposedly to the place of crucifixion and the place of the holy sepulchre. But all of this, according to tradition, we felt, was in the wrong place. We felt none of the spiritual significance which we had felt at other places. . . .
>
> There was yet another place we had to visit, the garden tomb. . . . Here our guide took us as though it were an afterthought, and as the woman guide with her little son led us through the garden, we saw a hill outside the gate of the walled city of Jerusalem, just a short way from where the hall of judgment had been inside the city walls. The garden was right close by, or "in the hill," as John had said, and in it was a sepulchre hewn out of a rock, evidently done by someone who could afford the expense of excellent workmanship.
>
> Something seemed to impress us as we stood there that this was the holiest place of all, and we fancied we

could have witnessed the dramatic scene that took place there. ("I Walked Today Where Jesus Walked," 6)

In 1979 President Spencer W. Kimball said of his visit to the Garden Tomb: "We accept this as the burial place of the Savior. We realize people have different ideas about these places, but this seems to be the logical place. I feel quite sure that this is the place where His body was laid. It gives me such a sacred feeling just to be here. I've preached quite a few sermons about this spot" (*Church News*, 3 November 1979, 5).

Just a few years ago, in a video presentation entitled *Special Witnesses of Christ*, President Gordon B. Hinckley said the following as he stood at the Garden Tomb: "Just outside the walls of Jerusalem, in this place or somewhere nearby was the tomb of Joseph of Arimathea, where the body of the Lord was interred."

Critical Issues

As most authorities acknowledge, ultimately it does not matter very much *where* Jesus was buried; rather, it does matter a great deal *why* and for *how long* he was buried and *what* happened in the tomb. A venerable instructor said to me once, when teaching with great power, "Suppose someone very dear to you died and was buried, but you did not know the location of the gravesite. And then suppose that after a few days, in the midst of your sadness, you saw this person walking toward you— fully alive. It is unlikely your first impulse would be to run about checking for the location of the grave to make sure it was really empty! Without a doubt your first impulse would be to run and embrace your loved one and revel in a joy as great as, or even greater than, was your sadness. If, therefore, you do not find the exact location of the Garden Tomb, revel in the joy of having found him who originally occupied the grave but now has left the tomb forevermore."

This does not mean that modern disciples should not be interested at all in the exact location of Golgotha and the Garden Tomb, places of such monumental import for the history of the world. But we ought to prayerfully consider the sacred texts describing the final moments of the Master's ministry, as well as the statements of the living witnesses, as our foundation, and then review the best analysis scholarship has to offer.

Another point of discussion that has arisen in the last few years centers on the nature of Jesus' sepulchre, particularly its size but also the type of stone used to seal it. Some authorities assert that because 98 percent of the Jewish tombs discovered by archaeologists in and around Jerusalem dating to the Second Temple period were sealed with square stones or plugs, and because the Greek verb *kulio,* translated in Matthew and Mark as "rolled," can also mean "moved," it is likely that the tomb of Jesus was sealed with a square stone and not a round, or a rolling, stone. Thus, these authorities argue, passages in the Gospels in the King James Version stating that the stone used to seal the tomb was "rolled" into place should be retranslated as "moved" into place. Furthermore, they assert, Jesus' tomb was of the standard small variety with a small entrance or opening (Kloner, "Did a Rolling Stone Close Jesus' Tomb?" 23–27).

In my view, the latest theories of archaeologists should not automatically be preferred over the actual wording of the King James New Testament. First, even though the actual number is very small, there are examples of tombs from the period in question that used round or disk-shaped stones to seal the entrance. These blocking stones are large, at least four feet in diameter, and the tombs that they sealed housed the wealthy and influential members of society (Herod's family tomb and the tombs of the kings are examples). In fact, round blocking stones "appeared only in the tombs of the wealthiest Jews" (Kloner, "Did a Rolling Stone Close Jesus' Tomb?" 28).

Second, both Matthew 27:60 and Mark 15:46 use the verb *kulindo*, which does not denote in its primary or secondary definitions the meaning "to move." It means "to roll." If Matthew and Mark didn't mean that the stone was rolled into place, why didn't they use a verb that did not carry so strongly the connotation of rolling or circular movement? (Remember, the Joseph Smith Translation does *not* change the text when it says the stone was "rolled" into place—though it does change other small points.) Isn't it possible that Matthew and Mark are actually saying what they really mean? Given that Joseph of Arimathea was a rich as well as an influential man and that the few rolling-stone tombs unearthed by archaeologists were *only* for the wealthy and influential, isn't it possible that the Garden Tomb of Jesus—Joseph's own intended tomb—was sealed with a rolling stone and that Jesus really was buried as a king in every way, including even the type and size of his sepulchre?

In the end, the New Testament leaves us with the most important information and lasting impressions about the site of our Savior's burial:

1. In the place where Jesus was crucified was a garden (John 19:41).

2. In the garden was a sepulchre (John 19:41). That the Savior's tomb was located in a real garden and not in an overgrown weed patch, as some have argued, is confirmed by Mary Magdalene on the first Easter morning when she initially supposed she was talking to the "gardener" (John

20:15). She was, of course, talking to *the* gardener—the Gardener of the Father's vineyard. But John's report was not metaphoric.

3. The tomb was new; no corpse had ever been placed there before (John 19:41; Luke 23:53).

4. The site of the tomb, and hence of the Crucifixion, was very close to the city (John 19:20).

5. The place of crucifixion (and of the tomb) was within moderate calling distance of the road. People passing by the site derided the Savior on the cross (Matthew 27:39; Mark 15:29). Bystanders misunderstood the Savior and thought he was calling to Elijah. In fact, what he said was, "Eli, Eli . . . My God, my God" (Matthew 27:46–47; Mark 15:34–35).

6. The tomb was hewn out of the rock; it was not a natural cave, and it cost its owner a fair amount (Matthew 27:60; Mark 15:46; Luke 23:53).

7. The tomb was closed up by rolling a *great* stone in front of the door (Matthew 27:60; Mark 15:46; 16:4), implying that the tomb was a rolling-stone tomb, the kind used by the wealthy and influential members of society, and that the stone was large.

8. The tomb was opened when the great stone was rolled back from the door by an earthquake and two angels (JST Matthew 28:2), also indicating that the stone was very large (Mark 16:4) and could keep the tomb secure.

9. The entrance of the tomb was low-cut; one had to stoop to look in (Luke 24:4; John 20:5).

10. The interior of the tomb, however, was large enough that

people could stand inside (Mark 16:5; Luke 24:3–4; John 20:6, 8). It was the family tomb of a wealthy man (Matthew 27:57).

As anyone knows who has ever laid a loved one to rest, it is comforting to have a befitting gravesite available for the deceased. All disciples of the Savior, ancient and modern, may be grateful that a man of the stature of Joseph of Arimathea was raised up to provide, at great personal sacrifice, a tomb fit for the King of heaven and earth. Isaiah had prophesied that the Messiah would be "with the rich in his death" (Isaiah 53:9), and so he was. Once Jesus' body had been laid to rest, Joseph "rolled a great stone to the door of the sepulchre, and departed" (Matthew 27:60).

On the Sabbath After the Crucifixion

Of all the Lord's disciples, the women (including those from Galilee) bore the brunt of the Lord's death. Most of the other disciples were not at the cross; they had fled. In addition, Luke's Gospel indicates that after Jesus' interment, the women returned to their places of abode to prepare additional burial spices and ointments because they had agreed to meet again at the tomb after the Sabbath and administer final burial preparations to the Savior's body in anticipation of a long entombment. And yet, though they may have been anxious to complete the burial procedures, they kept the Sabbath! Their reason for observing the day of rest was that it was the commandment of the Mosaic law, and they were obedient (Luke 23:56). They obeyed with exactness even when circumstances were at their worst.

Such faithfulness in the face of such a monumental loss is humbling, especially when we consider that their supposed "day of rest" could have been anything but restful for these sisters. The anguish of the previous day would have remained constant in their minds and hearts. They would have remembered every gory detail. We turn to an account from one who was at Nauvoo when Joseph and Hyrum Smith were murdered in order to understand more fully how overpoweringly vivid the Savior's death scene became for those early disciples who were at the cross. From Lyman Omer Littlefield we learn:

> The bodies of Joseph and Hyrum were brought to Nauvoo, dressed and laid in state at the Mansion House, where thousands of people, bathed in tears, passed in procession, two abreast, to view their mangled remains. The writer of this, with his wife, thus had the mournful privilege of looking one sad and brief adieu upon the noble forms of those men of God.
>
> That was an hour marked in the history of this people, and although forty-four years have since passed away, the powers of memory seldom go back and review the scene—though in gleams of momentary fleetness— without sensations of pain. (*Reminiscences of Latter-day Saints*, 162–63)

The Lord's disciples would never forget the events of what the world now calls Good Friday. It seems unlikely, however, that any of the disciples the following Saturday would have found anything good about it. Yet, as Joseph of Egypt had testified more than a thousand years earlier, God turns bad things into good. "But as for you, ye thought evil against me; but God meant it unto good, to bring to pass, as it is this day, to save much people alive" (Genesis 50:20). Isn't this the essence of the Atonement, a capsulized summary of the Savior's suffering? Though some thought evil against Jesus' life and ministry, God meant it unto good, to save much people alive! Truly, the life of Joseph of Egypt was itself a foreshadowing of the life and mission of the Messiah.

In stark contrast to the strict obedience manifested by Jesus' disciples on the day after His crucifixion, Matthew describes the continuing evil activity of the self-same religious leaders who were charged with ensuring that the Sabbath, as well as all other requirements of the Law, were complied with. They themselves violated the Sabbath by going to Pilate to request that a guard be placed at the tomb. At least two reasons made this extraordinary action necessary, although the Jewish leaders mentioned only one.

First, as they indicated, they were concerned that the disciples of Jesus might steal his body to make it appear as though he had risen from the dead. "Now the next day, that followed the day of the preparation, the chief priests and Pharisees came together unto Pilate, saying, Sir, we remember that that deceiver said, while he was yet alive, After three days I will rise again. Command therefore that the sepulchre be made sure until the third day, lest his disciples come by night, and steal him away, and say unto the people, He is risen from the dead: so the last error shall be worse than the first" (Matthew 27:62–64). In other words, from their point of view, any attempts by the disciples to validate Jesus' predictions about his own resurrection three days after his death would be worse than the predictions themselves. It is noteworthy that the Jewish leaders were quite conscious of Jesus' predictions about his own resurrection (Matthew 27:63).

A second reason why religious leaders wanted a guard posted went unspoken. Jesus had been an extremely popular figure with certain segments of the populace. Some of these segments resided in Galilee—Jesus' home district—and Galilee was already known as a hotbed of messianic expectation and zealot unrest! "When the news of his death became known and the Sabbath came to an end, would there be a popular outpouring of grief—or worse, of anger? A few days earlier those same religious authorities had been fearful of how the crowds would react if Jesus were arrested (Mark 14:2; Luke 22:2). We can imagine they might now have been even more fearful, when it became public knowledge that he had been arrested *and* put to death" (Walker, *Weekend That Changed the World*, 43–44).

Thus, Jewish leaders had no qualms about going to Pilate, a Gentile leader, on the day after the Crucifixion, a special and most sacred Sabbath day (John 19:31). Ultimately, they wanted to guarantee the secrecy of their conspiracy to have Jesus murdered and ensure the success of showing him to be a false messiah, even though it brought upon them ritual defilement according to their own tradition (McConkie, *Doctrinal New Testament Commentary*, 1:838).

The stage was now set for the earthshaking events of the next day. As Sunday approached, the women disciples were preparing to return to the tomb. The Jewish religious leaders had extracted permission from the Roman authorities to have guards keep the tomb rock-solid secure. "Two groups of guards (no doubt tired after the demanding activities of this Passover weekend) [were] beginning their night watch and waiting eagerly for daylight when their shift would be complete" and the world could begin to forget about the prophet from Galilee (Walker, *Weekend That Changed the World*, 45).

Little did anyone realize what lay ahead.

Now, concerning the state of the soul between death and the resurrection—Behold, it has been made known unto me by an angel, that the spirits of all men, as soon as they are departed from this mortal body, yea, the spirits of all men, whether they be good or evil, are taken home to that God who gave them life.

ALMA 40:11

CHAPTER 2

While His Body Lay in the Tomb

The moment after Jesus took his final breath, his immortal spirit left his physical body and entered a different dimension of eternal existence—the spirit world. Like every other person who has ever died, Jesus did not cease to exist when his physical body stopped functioning. The real Jesus continued to live. As with each one of us, the real Jesus had been a spirit being before he came to this earth, clothed with a spirit body that will never cease to exist—never cease to function. In fact, Joseph Smith consistently taught that our spirits are eternal. In 1833 the Lord revealed to the Prophet that "man was also in the beginning with God. Intelligence, or the light of truth, was not created or made, neither indeed can be. . . . For man is spirit. The elements are eternal" (D&C 93:29–30, 33). In 1839 Joseph taught that "the Spirit of Man is not a created being; it existed from Eternity & will exist to eternity. . . . earth, water, &c.—all these had their existence in an elementary State from Eternity" (Ehat and Cook, *Words of Joseph Smith*, 9).

By 1844, the Prophet's understanding of man's nature had been refined to the point where he could deliver his magnificent

King Follett Discourse, in which he spoke at length about the eternal existence of spirits:

> We say that God himself is a self-existent being. Who told you so? It is correct enough; but how did it get into your heads? Who told you that man did not exist in like manner upon the same principles? Man does exist upon the same principles. God made a tabernacle and put a spirit into it, and it became a living soul. . . . How does it read in the Hebrew? It does not say in the Hebrew that God created the spirit of man. It says "God made man out of the earth and put into him Adam's spirit, and so became a living body."
>
> The mind or the intelligence which man possesses is co-equal [co-eternal] with God himself. I know that my testimony is true; hence, when I talk to these mourners, what have they lost? Their relatives and friends are only separated from their bodies for a short season: their spirits which existed with God have left the tabernacle of clay only for a little moment, as it were; and they now exist in a place where they converse together the same as we do on the earth.
>
> I am dwelling on the immortality of the spirit of man. Is it logical to say that the intelligence of spirits is immortal, and yet that it had a beginning? The intelligence of spirits had no beginning, neither will it have an end. That is good logic. That which has a beginning may have an end. There never was a time when there were not spirits; for they are co-equal [co-eternal] with our Father in heaven. (*Teachings of the Prophet Joseph Smith*, 352–53)

Not only is Jesus' spirit eternal, as is each of ours, but it is composed of actual matter; it is elemental. It has size, shape, and occupies space. Again, the Prophet Joseph Smith revealed: "There is no such thing as immaterial matter. All spirit is matter, but it is more fine or pure, and can only be discerned by purer eyes; we cannot see it; but when our bodies are purified we shall see that it is all matter" (D&C 131:7–8). Elder Parley P. Pratt taught, "The spirit of man consists of an organization of the elements of spiritual matter in the likeness and after the pattern of the fleshly tabernacle." In fact, he expressed his conviction that the spirit body possesses "all the organs and parts exactly corresponding to the outward tabernacle" (*Key to the Science of Theology,* 79).

Elder Pratt's conviction is in perfect harmony with the revealed word of God as found in restoration scripture. Our physical bodies are created in the exact image of the bodies of our heavenly parents—male and female (Moses 6:8–9; Abraham 4:27). And our spirit bodies are in the likeness of our physical bodies, each possessing the corresponding features, organs, and parts of the other. This was true for Jesus, and it is true for us (Ether 3:15–16).

Thus, in the world of spirits after his mortal death, Jesus possessed form and substance, consciousness and sentience (ability to think and feel), volition (ability to choose and act), and accountability (obligation to face the consequences of his thoughts and actions), just as each of us will. We will find that after this life there is more life and more insight about life. Jesus' spirit body had the same form and features as his physical body, and so does each of ours. President Joseph Fielding Smith declared: "When the Lord appeared to the brother of Jared, he showed him his body. It was the body of his Spirit, and it was in the exact form of his tabernacle when he walked the streets and highways of Palestine" (*Answers to Gospel Questions,* 1:8).

TAKEN HOME TO GOD

When human beings die and their physical bodies cease to function, their spirits go to the world of spirits to await the time of reuniting with their physical bodies. This was true for Jesus. The Book of Mormon prophet Alma taught this doctrine in these words: "Now, concerning the state of the soul between death and the resurrection—Behold, it has been made known unto me by an angel, that the spirits of all men, as soon as they are departed from this mortal body, yea, the spirits of all men, whether they be good or evil, are taken home to that God who gave them life" (Alma 40:11).

Some misunderstandings have arisen over Alma's phrase "taken home to that God who gave them life" and require a little explanation. Several of the earlier apostles and prophets of this present dispensation have helped clarify the picture. To be taken home to God does not mean that each spirit will be immediately ushered into God's physical presence but rather that it will go into the spirit world, which is under His ultimate direction and control. Elder Orson Pratt indicated that the phrase "presence of God" does not necessarily require a close spatial relationship: "What are we to understand by being in the presence of God? Is it necessary to . . . be in the same vicinity or within a few yards or feet of him? I think not" (*Journal of Discourses,* 16:364–65).

Perhaps the clearest interpretation of Alma's use of the phrase "taken home to that God who gave them life" has been

38

proffered by President George Q. Cannon, counselor in the First Presidency for many years:

> Alma, when he says that "the spirits of all men, as soon as they are departed from this mortal body, . . . are taken home to that God who gave them life," has the idea, doubtless, in his mind that our God is omni-present—not in His own personality but through His minister, the Holy Spirit.
>
> He does not intend to convey the idea that they are immediately ushered into the personal presence of God. He evidently uses that phrase in a qualified sense. Solomon . . . makes a similar statement: "Then shall the dust return to the earth as it was: and the spirit shall return unto God who gave it." (Ecclesiastes 12:7.) The same idea is frequently expressed by the Latter-day Saints. In referring to a departed one it is often said that he has gone back to God, or he has gone "home to that God who gave him life." Yet it would not be contended that the person who said this meant that the departed one had gone where God, the Father Himself is, in the sense in which the Savior meant when He spake to Mary. (*Gospel Truth*, 58).

President Heber C. Kimball, also a counselor in the First Presidency in the nineteenth century, added the important insight that to enjoy the literal, physical presence of God the Father on a continuing basis, one must be a resurrected being, having one's spirit and body eternally reunited. Said he:

> As for my going into the immediate presence of God when I die, I do not expect it, but I expect to go into the

world of spirits and associate with my brethren, and preach the Gospel in the spiritual world, and prepare myself in every necessary way to receive my body again, and then enter through the wall [veil] into the celestial world. I never shall come into the presence of my Father and God until I have received my resurrected body, neither will any other person. (*Journal of Discourses,* 3:112–13)

What Heber C. Kimball taught is that in order to enter and stay in the literal, physical presence of God the Father, each of us *must* be a resurrected personage with a celestial body capable of enduring the Father's environment. President Kimball probably learned this doctrine from the Prophet of the Restoration, who taught that we prepare for God's presence "by going from one small degree to another, and from a small capacity to a great one; from grace to grace, from exaltation to exaltation, until [we] attain to the resurrection of the dead, and are able to dwell in everlasting burnings, and to sit in glory, as do those who sit enthroned in everlasting power" (*Teachings of the Prophet Joseph Smith,* 346–47).

This does not mean that God the Father cannot and does not visit nonresurrected beings for brief periods from time to time. Joseph Smith is a case in point. But in order for us to come into the Father's presence and live with him, we must be resurrected beings able to live in "everlasting burnings."

That brings us back to another part of Heber C. Kimball's statement, namely, that the spirit world is a place where we continue to associate with each other and prepare to receive again our physical bodies. The kind of body with which we are resurrected (celestial, terrestrial, or telestial) depends on the kind of spirit son or daughter we have developed into. A telestial spirit cannot be resurrected with a celestial body.

This statement of President Heber C. Kimball is in perfect harmony with Jesus' own experience and helps to explain the Savior's statement to Mary Magdalene on the morning of his resurrection. As she came forward to embrace him as a newly resurrected Being, he said to her, "Touch me not; for I am not yet ascended to my Father: but go to my brethren, and say unto them, I ascend unto my Father, and your Father; and to my God, and your God" (John 20:17). To be sure, there was now a special divine dignity attached to the Savior that discouraged too much familiarity. But more important, "no human hand was to be permitted to touch the Lord's resurrected and immortalized body until after He had presented Himself to the Father" (Talmage, *Jesus the Christ*, 682). Jesus had entered the spirit world as the disembodied Son of God, but he did not then enjoy the personal company and physical presence of his Father, our Father in Heaven. That came after he was resurrected.

NEARNESS OF THE SPIRIT WORLD

From several sources, then, we learn that the spirits of those who have passed through the veil at the time of death (Jesus included) go to the spirit world but not immediately into the physical presence of God. The patriarch Abraham beheld our physical universe and saw that the throne of God is an actual place in the universe, near a celestial orb named Kolob. More than that, other prophets have seen that the spirit world itself is also an actual location in the universe, but that it is right here on this earth! President Brigham Young taught this doctrine straightforwardly: "When you lay down this tabernacle, where are you going? Into the spiritual world. . . . Where is the spirit world? It is right here. Do the good and evil spirits go together? Yes they do. Do they go beyond the boundaries of this organized earth? No they do not" (*Journal of Discourses*, 3:368).

Jesus never left this earth when he entered the spirit world. While his body was laid to rest *in* the earth, Jesus' spirit entered a different realm of existence *on* the earth. By the time of his resurrection, Jesus had not yet been with his Father physically because his Father resided in a different locale as a glorified, divine Man with a body of flesh and bone (D&C 130:2–22). Certainly Jesus felt the influence of his Father as he resided in the spirit world.

Elder Parley P. Pratt taught that the spirit world for the inhabitants of this earth is located on this earth. But he also implied that the spirit worlds for the other planets like our own are located on those other planets. Said he:

> As to its location [the spirit world], it is here on the very planet where we were born; or, in other words, the earth and other planets of a like sphere, have their inward or spiritual spheres, as well as their outward, or temporal. The one is peopled by temporal tabernacles, and the other by spirits. A veil is drawn between the one sphere and the other, whereby all the objects in the spiritual sphere are rendered invisible to those in the temporal. (*Key to the Science of Theology*, 80)

We do not know when Jesus visited the spirit worlds of all his creations, but I am inclined to view the report of his visit to the spirits in prison recorded in Doctrine and Covenants 138 as referring to this earth only. Nonetheless, just as we know he visits each of his kingdoms in due season, we also believe he did or will visit each spirit world in its appropriate season. The parable of the lord of the fields, which describes the owner or lord of many fields visiting each and every field, "beginning at the first, and so on unto the last," is recorded in Doctrine and Covenants 88:51–61. In my view, it may be applied to the spirit worlds of every earth. Regarding the meaning of this parable, Elder Orson Pratt said that the Lord "has other worlds or creations and other sons and daughters, perhaps just as good as those dwelling on this planet, and they, as well as we, will be visited, and they will be made glad with the countenance of their Lord" (*Journal of Discourses*, 17:332). More important, the Lord not only visits all of the worlds he created but he redeems each and every one through the infinite power of his atonement (D&C 76:22–24, 41–42).

The Prophet Joseph Smith knew that the spirit world was very close. In fact, regarding the spirits of the righteous, he said not only are they "not far from us" but they "know and understand our thoughts, feelings, and motions, and are often pained therewith" (*Teachings of the Prophet Joseph Smith*, 326). Because of the nearness of the world of spirits, and their cognizance of and sensitivity to our circumstances in mortality, mortals are sometimes accorded the privilege of receiving visitations from those beings of the unseen world of spirits, if such visits are in harmony with the mind and will of the Lord.

During the Lord's earthly ministry, his apostles manifested their belief in visitations from disembodied spirits (Matthew 14:26; Luke 24:37). After his resurrection, when they began to lead the Church and leave written testimonies for the Saints, the apostles came to know the living reality of beings from the unseen world. They understood the nature of visitations by spirits to Mary, Joseph, and others (Luke 1:19). They themselves communed with angels and spirit beings as a natural course of events. They were saved from harm by them and testified of their reality (Acts 1:11; 5:19; Jude 1:6). New Testament records leave no doubt that spirits and angels worked with mortals in the meridian dispensation.

In our present dispensation, the dispensation of the fulness of times, apostles and prophets have also testified of the reality of visitations by spirits from the world beyond. Some examples may be instructive as well as fortifying, serving to strengthen our testimonies of the reality of life beyond the grave.

The Prophet Joseph Smith was visited by both resurrected beings and the spirits of just men made perfect, and he knew others were and would be visited as well. He said: "There are two kinds of beings in heaven, namely: Angels, who are resurrected personages, having bodies of flesh and bones—For instance, Jesus said: Handle me and see, for a spirit hath not flesh and bones, as ye see me have. Secondly: the spirits of just men made perfect, they who are not resurrected, but inherit the same glory" (D&C 129:1–3). Therefore, the Prophet presented significant instructions on how to discern the type of messenger with whom one was communicating—angels, the spirits of just men made perfect, or the devil (D&C 129:4–9). In 1843 he commented that "the spirits of just men are made ministering servants to those who are sealed unto life eternal. . . . Patriarch [James] Adams is now one of the spirits of the just men made perfect. . . . Angels [resurrected beings] have advanced higher in knowledge and power than spirits" (*Teachings of the Prophet Joseph Smith*, 325).

Elder Parley P. Pratt, a spiritual giant himself, knew a great deal about the spirit world. He taught:

Persons who have departed this life and have not yet been raised from the dead are spirits. These are of two kinds: good and evil.

These two kinds also include many grades of good and evil.

The good spirits, in the superlative sense of the word, are they who, in this life, partook of the Holy Priesthood and of the fulness of the gospel. This class of spirits minister to the heirs of salvation, both in this world and in the world of spirits. They can appear unto men when permitted. (*Key to the Science of Theology*, 71–72)

President Wilford Woodruff, fourth president of the Church, bore a powerful witness of ministrations from those who had passed on:

Joseph Smith visited me a great deal after his death, and taught me many important principles. On one occasion he and his brother Hyrum visited me while I was in a storm at sea. . . . The night following [the storm at sea] Joseph and Hyrum visited me, and the Prophet laid before me a great many things. Among other things he told me to get the Spirit of God; that all of us needed it. . . .

Joseph Smith continued visiting myself and others up to a certain time, and then it stopped. The last time I saw him . . . [he] came to me and spoke to me. He said he could not stop to talk with me because he was in a hurry. . . . I met half a dozen brethren who had held high positions on earth, and none of them could stop to talk with me because they were in a hurry. I was much astonished. (*Discourses of Wilford Woodruff*, 288–89).

On another occasion President Woodruff commented about visitations from the spirit world:

> I believe the eyes of the heavenly hosts are over this people; I believe they are watching the elders of Israel, the prophets and apostles and men who are called to bear off this kingdom. I believe they watch over us all with great interest. . . .
>
> I have had many interviews with Brother Joseph until the last 15 or 20 years of my life; I have not seen him for that length of time. But during my travels in the southern country last winter I had many interviews with President Young, and with Heber C. Kimball, and Geo. A. Smith, and Jedediah M. Grant, and many others who are dead. They attended our conference, they attended our meetings.
>
> And on one occasion, I saw Brother Brigham and Brother Heber ride in [a] carriage ahead of the carriage in which I rode when I was on my way to attend conference; and they were dressed in the most priestly robes. When we arrived at our destination I asked Prest. Young if he would preach to us. He said, "No, I have finished my testimony in the flesh. I shall not talk to this people any more. But (said he) I have come to see you; I have come to watch over you, and to see what the people are doing. Then, said he, I want you to teach the people— and I want you to follow this counsel yourself—that they must labor and so live as to obtain the Holy Spirit, for without this you cannot build up the kingdom; without

the spirit of God you are in danger of walking in the dark, and in danger of failing to accomplish your calling as apostles and as elders in the church and kingdom of God. And, said he, Brother Joseph taught me this principle. And I will here say, I have heard him refer to that while he was living. . . .

The thought came to me that Brother Joseph had left the work of watching over this church and kingdom to others, and that he had gone ahead, and that he had left this work to men who have lived and labored with us since he left us. This idea manifested itself to me, that such men advance in the spirit world. And I believe myself that these men who have died and gone into the spirit world had this mission left with them, that is, a certain portion of them, to watch over the Latter-day Saints. (*Journal of Discourses*, 21:317–18; paragraphing altered)

Closer to our day, we have the testimony of apostles and prophets who have certified to us that beings from the spirit world do return to offer instruction and encouragement. At the funeral of President Ezra Taft Benson, President Boyd K. Packer spoke of the spirit world:

Now this dear, venerable prophet has entered in, there to rejoice with his beloved Flora and to speak of their wonderful family, there to rejoice with Joseph and Brigham and John and Wilford and the others.

The prophets who preceded him, ancient and modern, have on occasion communed with the servants of the Lord on this earth. So it well may be that we have not seen the last of this great prophet of God.

I testify that the veil between this mortal realm and the spirit world opens to such revelation and visitation as the needs of the church and kingdom of God on earth may require. ("We Honor Now His Journey," 34).

In addition to apostles and prophets, other righteous men, women, and children have been privileged to enjoy visitations from those residing temporarily in the spirit world. Andrew C. Nelson, a stalwart member of the Church living at the close of the nineteenth century, recorded such an experience in his journal. He was visited by his father shortly after his father's death:

On the night of April 6th, 1891, I had a strange dream or vision in which I saw and conversed with my father who died January 27th, 1891. . . .

Though some may scorn and laugh at the idea of such a visitation, yet I feel assured that it was real, and it has been and I hope always will be a source of much pleasure and satisfaction to me. To corroborate my testimony of the possibility of such a visitation I quote the following: "Spirits can appear to men when permitted; but not having a fleshy tabernacle can not hide their glory." [*Key to Theology*, p. 120.] I was in bed when father came in or entered the room; he came and sat on the side of the bed. . . .

When father came to the bed, he first said: "Well, my son, being you were not there (at Redmond) when I died, so that I did not get to see you, and as I had a few spare minutes, I received permission to come and see you a few minutes." "I am very glad to see you father. How do you do?" "I am feeling well my son, and have had very much to do since I died."

"What have you been doing since you died father? . . ."

. . . "My son, I have been travelling together with Apostle Erastus Snow ever since I died; that is, since three days after I died; then I received my commission to preach the Gospel. You can not imagine, my son, how many spirits there are in the Spirit world that have not yet received the Gospel; but many are receiving it, and a great work is being accomplished. Many are anxiously looking forth to their friends, who are still living, to administer for them in the Temples. I have been very busy in preaching the Gospel of Jesus Christ."

"Will all the spirits believe you, father, when you teach them the Gospel?" "No, they will not." . . .

"Father, can you see us at all times, and do you know what we are doing?" "No, my son, I can not. I have something else to do. I can not go when and where I please. There is just as much, and much more, order here in the Spirit world than in the other world. I have been assigned work and that must be performed." . . .

"How do you feel at all times, father?" "O, I feel splendid, and enjoy my labors, still, I must admit that at times I get a little lonesome to see my family; but it is only a short time till we will again see each other." . . .

"Father, is it natural to die? or does it seem natural? Was there not a time when your spirit was in such a pain that it could not realize what was going on or taking place?" "No, my son, there was not such a time. It is just as natural to die, as it is to be born, or for you to pass out of that door (here he pointed at the door). When I had told the folks that I could not last long, it turned dark and I could not see anything for a few minutes. Then, the first thing I could see was a number of spirits in the Spirit world. Then, I told the folks that I must go. . . ."

"Father, is the principle and doctrine of the Resurrection as taught us true?" "True. Yes, my son, as true as can be. You can not avoid being Resurrected. It is just as natural for all to be Resurrected as it is to be born and die again. No one can avoid being Resurrected. There are many spirits in the Spirit world who would to God that there would be no Resurrection."

"Father, is the Gospel as taught by this Church true?" "My son, do you see that picture?" (pointing to a picture of the First Presidency of the Church hanging on the wall) "Yes, I see it." "Well, just as sure as you see that picture, just so sure is the Gospel true. The Gospel of Jesus Christ has within it the power of saving every man and woman that will obey it, and in no other way can they ever obtain a salvation in the Kingdom of God." (Nelson, *From Heart to Heart*, 16–17)

INTEREST IN US

There is no doubt that beings from the unseen world of spirits can and do visit righteous mortals from all walks of life and stations in the Church, from prophets to Primary children. The spirits who return are part of that category of beings we call angels (both resurrected and not yet resurrected) who are promised to all the Saints, especially missionaries, as they go forth to do the Lord's work. Often the term *angels* is used to refer to resurrected beings, but sometimes it includes spirits not yet resurrected: "Behold, I [the Lord] send you out to reprove the world of all their unrighteous deeds. . . . And whoso receiveth you, there I will be also. . . . I will be on your right hand and on your left, . . . *and mine angels* round about you, to bear you up" (D&C 84:87–88; emphasis added). Most often these angels (resurrected beings and righteous spirits) from beyond the veil do not make dramatic appearances to us but are there helping us along, as President George Q. Cannon testified: "But there are also angels around us. Though invisible to us they are continually inviting us and pleading with us to do that which is right. The Spirit of God, too, rests upon us, and it prompts us to keep the commandments of God. By means of these influences, therefore, we are receiving experience and we are growing in knowledge" (*Gospel Truth*, 66).

From a great many witnesses we learn that the spirits of the righteous have a genuine interest in the progress and welfare of those in mortality. It seems to me that these ministering angels and spirits are as likely as not to be members of one's own family or one's circle of friends in mortality. They aid us in our missionary work as well as our family history research and temple work. They know us and know best how to help us. Their experiences and activities are very much like our own activities on this side of the veil. They yearn to be reunited with their family and friends. The same sociality which exists among us here on this side of the veil exists among them on that side of the veil (D&C 130:2). Beings in the spirit world may even pray for the health and happiness of us mortals.

The experience of one of my own family members taught her that those on the other side of the veil can and do pray for us on this side and that she herself was prayed for at a difficult time in her life by family members who had gone before her. She learned this by personal revelation. In her history she tells of the death of her nineteen-year-old daughter and of being "frantic with grief." She was nearly devastated. She had already lost another child years earlier. In that moment of her extremity, a vision opened to her. She saw departed loved ones on the other side of the veil praying for her. Just as important, her personal record of this and other experiences has taught her descendants valuable lessons about life beyond the veil. As the Prophet Joseph Smith said, the spirit world is very near.

It is also true that inhabitants of the spirit world are themselves, in turn, ministered to by servants of God. "Angels [meaning resurrected beings in this case] are ministers both to men upon the earth and to the world of spirits. They pass from one world to another with more ease and in less time than we pass from one city to another" (Pratt, *Key to the Science of Theology*, 69). All of this is according to our Heavenly Father's watchful care over his children on both sides of the veil and is made possible by the very atoning act that had brought Jesus to the spirit world.

Therefore, when Jesus entered the spirit world and began the next phase of his foreordained mission and ministry, he did so as the great Liberator—the Bearer of light, life, and release to those who had been held captive by the bands of death since the time they themselves had passed through the veil. It is not hard to imagine that as he entered the world of spirits he was welcomed and hailed as the true King and God he really is by those righteous Saints whom he has known for eons. "While the corpse lay in Joseph's rock-hewn tomb, the living Christ existed as a disembodied Spirit. . . . He went where the spirits of the dead ordinarily go; and . . . in the sense in which while in the flesh He had been a Man among men, He was, in the disembodied state a Spirit among spirits" (Talmage, *Jesus the Christ*, 670).

And there were gathered together in one place an innumerable company of the spirits of the just, who had been faithful in the testimony of Jesus while they lived in mortality.

And there he preached to them the everlasting gospel, the doctrine of the resurrection and the redemption of mankind from the fall, and from individual sins on conditions of repentance.

And as I wondered, my eyes were opened, and my understanding quickened, and I perceived that the Lord went not in person among the wicked and the disobedient who had rejected the truth, to teach them;

But behold, from among the righteous, he organized his forces and appointed messengers, clothed with power and authority, and commissioned them to go forth and carry the light of the gospel to them that were in darkness, even to all the spirits of men; and thus was the gospel preached to the dead.

DOCTRINE AND COVENANTS 138:12, 19, 29–30

CHAPTER 3

His Ministry in the Spirit World

Just as death came to the Savior as a natural consequence of
mortality, so it comes to all people—not to punish but rather
"to fulfil the *merciful* plan of the great Creator" (2 Nephi 9:6;
emphasis added). Just as the transition from this world to the
next was immediate for the Savior, so it is for all people. Just as
the Savior did not leave this earth when he entered the spirit
world, so each one of us will go to that very same spirit world
that exists on this earth, whether we are male or female, good or
bad, old or young. We will not immediately all go to the same
part of the spirit world, however. When Jesus passed through the
veil, he entered a world of great division where the righteous
were *separated* from the wicked by a vast, unbridged gulf that had
been in place since the time of Adam.

A GREAT DIVISION

During his mortal ministry, Jesus had spoken of the great
division in the world of spirits. His best-known illustration of
that doctrine and reality came in the parable of the rich man and
Lazarus. A certain rich man, who lived in opulence, and a beggar

named Lazarus, who lived in abject poverty and misery, both died. The former looked up from hell (spirit prison) and saw Lazarus in Abraham's bosom (paradise). The rich man cried out to Father Abraham to send Lazarus to bring him some relief. Abraham responded by explaining that in the spirit world the law of complete justice holds sway (including equity, fairness, recompense for thoughts and deeds, and recompense for mortality's *injustices*). "Son, remember that thou in thy lifetime receivedst thy good things, and likewise Lazarus evil things: but now he is comforted, and thou art tormented" (Luke 16:25).

This part of the story simply reinforces what we already know about the lasting effects of the Savior's atonement: As a result of Gethsemane and Golgotha, justice becomes the friend of the righteous! All the injustices and unfairnesses of mortality are made up to the humble followers of Jesus—all of this world's inequities are made right and whole and fair for eternity. This is one of the most magnificent and gratitude-inspiring aspects of Jesus' unmatched act of love. If we honestly commit to follow him, he promises that the stain of our sins will be removed, and every pain, every sorrow, every sickness, every heartache not of our own making will be soothed and salved and healed. Every unfair circumstance of life will be made up to us. Our condition in eternity will not be determined by what happened *to* us but rather what will happen *in* us as a result of the Savior's atonement.

The other great lesson about life beyond our mortal probation comes in the next verse of the parable and illustrates the environment of the spirit world into which Jesus entered. "And beside all this," says Abraham to the rich man, "between us and you there is a *great gulf fixed:* so that they which would pass from hence to you cannot: neither can they pass to us, that would come from thence" (Luke 16:26; emphasis added). Of course, Lazarus and the rich man represent the two basic categories of people found in mortality (righteous and unrighteous), and the profound lesson of the parable focuses on their separation in the eternities, beginning in the spirit world. In the spirit world of Jesus' day, the great gulf prevented any social interchange between the righteous and the unrighteous. Elder Bruce R. McConkie further taught that the two groups of people, represented by the rich man and Lazarus "knew each other in mortality, so they remember their former acquaintanceship. But no longer are they accessible to each other so that one might minister to the needs of the other. Christ [had] not yet bridged the gulf between the prison and palace, and there [was] as yet no communion between the righteous in paradise and the wicked in hell" (*Mortal Messiah*, 3:263). Thus, the parable of the rich man and Lazarus not only illustrates the existence of a great division, including the idea that justice operates in the next life and that there is torment awaiting the wicked, but also the fact that each individual will remember the associations and experiences of this mortal life.

Long before the Savior taught and ministered personally on the earth as the mortal Messiah, Book of Mormon prophets spoke of the great division in the spirit world. Nephi, speaking almost six hundred years before the birth of Jesus, said of the fountain of filthy waters in his father's dream: "It was an awful gulf, which separated the wicked from the tree of life, and also from the saints of God" (1 Nephi 15:28). In this verse Nephi told his audience that the awful gulf not only separated the unrighteous from the righteous or "saints of God" but also that it separated the unrighteous from the tree of life, which is a symbol for Jesus Christ himself as Nephi learned earlier (1 Nephi 11:4–7,

9–22). Twenty-five hundred years later, another prophet, Joseph F. Smith, would receive a vision of the spirit world and see that Nephi was exactly right—the wicked in the world of spirits were never privileged to enjoy the physical presence of the Savior, nor hear his voice in person, when he entered the spirit world (D&C 138:20–21). The unrighteous were indeed separated from the tree of life by an awful gulf.

Centuries after Nephi, another Book of Mormon prophet, Alma, uttered what is arguably the classic statement on the great unbridged division that existed in the spirit world before the coming of Christ to the ranks of the disembodied spirits:

> And then shall it come to pass, that the spirits of those who are righteous are received into a state of happiness, which is called paradise, a state of rest, a state of peace, where they shall rest from all their troubles and from all care, and sorrow.
>
> And then shall it come to pass, that the spirits of the wicked, yea, who are evil—for behold, they have no part nor portion of the Spirit of the Lord; for behold, they chose evil works rather than good; therefore the spirit of the devil did enter into them, and take possession of their house—and these shall be cast out into outer darkness; there shall be weeping, and wailing, and gnashing of teeth, and this because of their own iniquity, being led captive by the will of the devil.
>
> Now this is the state of the souls of the wicked, yea, in darkness, and a state of awful, fearful looking for the fiery indignation of the wrath of God upon them; thus they remain in this state, as well as the righteous in

paradise, until the time of their resurrection. (Alma 40:12–14)

CONDITIONS IN THE TWO REALMS

Alma's discourse on the world of spirits is very helpful for its description of the spirit world when Jesus went there. The righteous lived in paradise—a state of happiness and peace, a place where, according to President Joseph F. Smith, they could "expand in wisdom, where they have respite from all their troubles, and where care and sorrow [did] not annoy" (*Gospel Doctrine*, 448). It truly was an environment where the hardships, struggles, and pains of mortality, especially those associated with the physical body, were left behind.

> Paradise is a place where the spirit is free to think and act with a renewed capacity and with the vigor and enthusiasm which characterized one in his prime. Though a person does not rest per se from the work associated with the plan of salvation (for . . . that labor goes forward with at least an equal intensity in the spirit world), at the same time he is delivered from those cares and worries associated with a fallen world and a corrupt body. (Millet and McConkie, *Life Beyond*, 18)

On the other hand, that part of the spirit world called hell or spirit prison was a place where there was weeping, hardship, and misery. Hell was and is both a place and a condition or state of mind. As the Prophet Joseph Smith explained, it is hell because of mental torment and anguish owing to disobedience and lack of repentance in mortality. "The great misery of departed spirits in the world of spirits, where they go after death, is to know that they come short of the glory that others enjoy and that they might have enjoyed themselves, and they are their own accusers" (*Teachings of the Prophet Joseph Smith*, 310–11). On another occasion the Prophet reinforced this doctrine by stating that "a man is his own tormentor and condemner. Hence the saying, They shall go in the lake that burns with fire and brimstone. The torment of disappointment in the mind of man is as exquisite as a lake burning with fire and brimstone" (*Teachings of the Prophet Joseph Smith*, 357).

Thus, those who were confined to that part of the spirit world known as spirit prison or hell, from Adam's day to the time when the Savior himself entered the spirit world, were awakened to a lively sense of their own guilt and shrank from the Spirit and presence of the Lord (Mosiah 2:38; Mormon 9:3–4). They themselves did not want, of their own free will and choice, to be in the presence of the temporarily disembodied Messiah, the Jehovah of earlier days, the man known as Jesus of Nazareth in the meridian dispensation. Hence, Jesus did not move among the wicked, did not have any interaction with them—both on account of *their* own desires as well as *his* own inability to look upon, to tolerate, to be in the presence of unrepented sin (D&C 1:31). The "damnation of hell," said Joseph Smith, is "to go with that society who have not obeyed His commands" (*Teachings of the Prophet Joseph Smith*, 198). The distasteful environment of hell is intensified precisely because a person is forced to dwell with other wicked and depraved individuals. Jesus had already experienced the environment of hell once before, during his time in Gethsemane. He would not go back.

DEATH—A PARTIAL JUDGMENT

At least three other significant implications of the doctrine of the great gulf or division in the spirit world are important to mention. First, the existence of the two separate places of abode for the spirits of the departed implies at least a partial judgment at the time of death. The disembodied spirits of all who have ever lived on the earth will receive a temporary inheritance in either paradise or spirit prison based on their actions in mortality. At the time of death each individual will be judged according to several factors. These include the following:

1. A person's accountability and age (Mosiah 3:16; Moroni 8:8–19); little children who die before they arrive at the years of accountability are saved automatically in the celestial kingdom of heaven (D&C 137:10)

2. The degree of knowledge individuals possessed, and their opportunity for righteous living during their mortal probation (Moroni 8:22; 2 Nephi 9:25–26)

3. A person's deeds, desires, and intents or motives (Mosiah 4:6; 1 Nephi 15:33; D&C 33:1; Alma 41:3; D&C 137:9)

4. Individuals' own acknowledgment of their true standing before the Lord—a self-judgment, if you will (2 Nephi 9:46; Mosiah 16:1; 27:31; 29:12)

Elder Bruce R. McConkie teaches an important concept when he speaks of death as a day of judgment:

> Death itself is an initial *day of judgment* for all persons, both the righteous and the wicked. When the spirit leaves the body at death, it is taken home to that God who gave it life, meaning that it returns to live in the realm of spiritual existence (Eccles. 17:7). At that time the spirit undergoes a partial judgment and is assigned an

inheritance in paradise or in hell to await the day of the first or second resurrection. (*Mormon Doctrine*, 402)

The second implication of the doctrine of a great gulf in the spirit world is the question of who is deemed righteous and who is not, and what the ultimate criteria are for determining who receives paradise and who does not. President Joseph Fielding Smith provides clear, invaluable commentary on this question:

It is the righteous who go to paradise. It is the righteous who cease from those things that trouble. Not so with the wicked. They remain in torment. . . . They are aware of their neglected opportunities, privileges in which they might have served the Lord and received a reward of restfulness. . . .

The righteous, *those who have kept the commandments* of the Lord, are not shut up in any such place, but are in happiness in paradise. . . .

All spirits of men after death return to the spirit world. There, as I understand it, *the righteous—meaning those who have been baptized and who have been faithful—* are gathered in one part and all the others in another part of the spirit world. (*Doctrines of Salvation*, 2:229–30; emphasis added)

Thus, President Smith cites two criteria which are the final or ultimate determiners of the destiny of the spirits of all men and women: keeping the commandments *and* participating in the ordinance of baptism. In other words, the righteous are those who had "been faithful in the testimony of Jesus while they lived in mortality; and who had offered sacrifice in the similitude of the great sacrifice of the Son of God, and suffered tribulation in their Redeemer's name" (D&C 138:12–13). The righteous in the spirit world are also referred to as "the spirits of the just" (D&C 138:12). They are those who lived the celestial law while in mortality. The ranks of the wicked on the other hand—those in spirit prison—are composed of men and women who lived a terrestrial or a telestial law in mortality. This includes those who died without knowing the law of the gospel or the truths of salvation; those who received not the testimony of Jesus in the flesh, but afterward received it; those who received not the gospel of Christ nor the testimony of Jesus at all; those thrust down to hell (D&C 76:72–84).

Even though there were good people living on the earth before the birth of Jesus, those who did not have the opportunity of hearing about the Messiah or accepting the gospel message had to wait in that part of the spirit world called spirit prison, or hell, until the arrival of the Savior in the spirit world made it possible for them to hear the gospel preached. Again, Elder McConkie corroborates that the circumstances or environment existing in the spirit world prior to the Savior's visit affected every person who had ever lived and died upon the earth:

> There was no intermingling by the spirits in paradise and hell until after Christ bridged the "great gulf" between these two spirit abodes (Alma 40:11–14). This he did while his body lay in the tomb of Joseph of Arimathea and his own disembodied spirit continued to minister to men in their spirit prison (1 Peter 3:18–21; 4:6; Joseph F. Smith, *Gospel Doctrine*, 5th ed., pp. 472–476). "Until that day" the prisoners remained bound and the gospel was not preached to them (Moses 7:37–39).

The hope of salvation for the dead was yet future. (*Doctrinal New Testament Commentary*, 1:521–22)

In truth, the term *prison*, though used to distinguish one part of the spirit world from the other part, called paradise, also applies to the whole of the spirit world. All of the spirit world is, in a sense, a prison. This is true because the spirits of *both* the righteous and the wicked are separated from their physical bodies, and to be without one's physical body is an intensely undesirable state of bondage. In the words of the revelation to President Joseph F. Smith: "For the dead [the righteous dead] had looked upon the long absence of their spirits from their bodies as a bondage" (D&C 138:50). So, even though the spirits of the righteous will be happy in paradise, they will not be, cannot be, perfectly happy while a part of them is lying in the grave. In the language of the revelations of the Restoration, the spirit and the body are the soul of man. When inseparably connected, the spirit and the physical body can receive a fulness of joy. When separated they cannot receive a fulness of joy (D&C 88:15; 93:33; 138:17). Without their physical bodies, the spirits of all men and women "are in prison," said President Brigham Young (*Journal of Discourses*, 3:95).

Elder Melvin J. Ballard gave this explanation:

I grant you that the righteous dead will be at peace, but I tell you that when we go out of this life, leave this body, we will desire to do many things that we cannot do at all without the body. We will be seriously handicapped, and we will long for the body; we will pray for the early reunion with our bodies. . . .

. . . we are sentencing ourselves to long periods of bondage, separating our spirits from our bodies, or we are shortening that period, according to the way in which we overcome and master ourselves [in mortality]. (Quoted in Hinckley, *Sermons and Missionary Services of Melvin Joseph Ballard*, 240–42)

This leads us to a third implication of the doctrine of the great gulf in the spirit world. It is significant that modern prophets and inspired teachers who have spoken about conditions extant in the spirit world not only talk about the great gulf or division of spirits *before* the Savior's visit but also speak of that division in the present tense. This is so because the great gulf, though bridged by the Savior for the first time when he visited the spirit world, still exists. The spirits of the wicked are still separated from the spirits of the righteous in our day, and that gulf is removed only by the preaching of the gospel and its acceptance by the spirits in spirit prison, or hell.

Concerning the environment that has existed in the spirit world since the Savior's liberating visit two thousand years ago, Elder Heber C. Kimball said: "Can those persons who pursue a course of carelessness, neglect of duty, and disobedience, when they depart from this life, expect that their spirits will associate with the spirits of the righteous in the spirit world? I do not expect it, and when you depart from this state of existence, you will find out for yourselves" (*Journal of Discourses*, 2:150).

Elder Parley P. Pratt likewise described the conditions of the spirit world all of us will encounter when we die:

> The spirit world is not the heaven where Jesus Christ, his Father, and other beings dwell who have, by resurrection or translation, ascended to eternal mansions and been crowned and seated on thrones of power; but it is an intermediate state, a probation, a place of

preparation, improvement, instruction, or education, where spirits are chastened and improved and where, if found worthy, they may be taught a knowledge of the gospel. In short, it is a place where the gospel is preached and where faith, repentance, hope, and charity may be exercised; a place of waiting for the resurrection or redemption of the body; while to those who deserve it, it is a place of punishment, a purgatory or hell, where spirits are buffeted till the day of redemption. (*Key to the Science of Theology*, 80)

No Need for the Righteous to Fear Death

Therefore, death holds no terror for those trying to keep God's commandments while living in mortality, trying to do as the Lord wants them to do. None of us need fear death. In making this point, President George Q. Cannon presented an extremely comforting picture of death for the righteous:

How delightful it is to contemplate the departure of those who have been faithful, as far as their knowledge permitted, to the truth which God has revealed! There is no sting nor gloom nor inconsolable sorrow about the departure of such persons. Holy angels are around their bedside to administer unto them. The Spirit of God rests down upon them, and His messengers are near them to introduce them to those who are on the other side of the veil. (*Gospel Truth*, 61)

President Cannon went on to state that Satan has no power

over the righteous dead—that is, those who have been baptized and have tried to live good lives in mortality:

> Satan is bound as soon as the faithful spirit leaves this tabernacle of clay and goes to the other side of the veil. That spirit is emancipated from the power and thraldom and attacks of Satan. Satan can only afflict such in this life. He can only afflict those in that life which is to come who have listened to his persuasions, who have listed to obey him. These are the only ones over whom he has power after this life. . . .
>
> They are his servants; they are under his influence. He takes possession of them when they pass from this mortal existence, and they experience the torments of hell. (*Gospel Truth*, 61)

In addition, for the righteous who pass through death, the spirit world will be a place of reunion, just as it surely was for Jesus when he entered the spirit world. Though we will undoubtedly miss our loved ones who are still living in mortality, paradise will be a time of happiness and excitement as we meet those who have gone before. The Prophet Joseph Smith taught this concept with assurance: "I have a father, brothers, children and friends who have gone to a world of spirits. They are only absent for a moment. They are in the spirit, and we shall soon meet again" (*Teachings of the Prophet Joseph Smith*, 359).

President Joseph F. Smith added this thought: "What is more desirable than that we should meet with our fathers and our mothers, with our brethren and our sisters, with our wives and our children, with our beloved associates and kindred in the spirit world, knowing each other, identifying each other . . . by the associations that familiarize each to the other in mortal life? What do you want better than that?" ("The Resurrection," 178)

Armed with this information, we find that death takes on a different perspective for all of us who are trying to be faithful, just as it did for those ancient righteous Saints in the spirit world two thousand years ago, awaiting the arrival of the Messiah. Because of the gospel of Jesus Christ, death loses its fearfulness.

It seems to me that this glorious truth cannot be emphasized enough. I wish I had understood it better at the time my own father died. I think my grieving would have been different. If we rely on the Savior and try to live good and decent lives in mortality, death actually becomes a blessing, a time of peace and rest, a time when physical pain and mortal cares cease, a time of reunion with those who have gone before us, a time of continuing intellectual and spiritual increase and development, a time when Satan is bound and can never again afflict or torment us, a time of great security. In fact, Elder Bruce R. McConkie spoke of life after death as a time when righteous individuals could no longer fall off the straight and narrow path. He said, in effect, there is no apostasy from paradise:

> In order to be saved in the Kingdom of God and in order to pass the test of mortality, what you have to do is get on the straight and narrow path—thus charging a course leading to eternal life—and then, being on that path, pass out of this life in full fellowship. . . . If you're on that path and pressing forward, and you die, you'll never get off the path. There is no such thing as falling off the straight and narrow path in the life to come, and the reason is that this life is the time that is given to men to prepare for eternity. . . . You don't have to live a life

that's truer than true. You don't have to have excessive zeal that becomes fanatical and becomes unbalancing. What you have to do is stay in the mainstream of the Church and live as upright and decent people live in the Church—keeping the commandments, paying your tithing, serving in the organizations of the Church, loving the Lord, staying on the straight and narrow path. If you're on that path when death comes—because this is the time and the day appointed, this the probationary estate—you'll never fall off from it, and, for all practical purposes, your calling and election is made sure. ("Probationary Test of Mortality," 219)

Not only is the spirit world a place of security for the righteous but it also is a place of great learning. Elder Orson Pratt of the Quorum of the Twelve (1811–81) spoke powerfully of the increased capacities of spirits in paradise to learn, grow intellectually, and increase in knowledge exponentially:

> When I speak of the future state of man, and the situation of our spirits between death and the resurrection, I long for the experience and knowledge to be gained in that state, as well as this. We shall learn many more things there; we need not suppose our five senses connect us with all the things of heaven, and earth, and eternity, and space; we need not think that we are conversant with all the elements of nature, through the medium of the senses God has given us here. Suppose He should give us a sixth sense, a seventh, an eighth, a ninth, or a fiftieth. All these different senses would convey to us new ideas, as much so as the senses of tasting,

smelling, or seeing communicate different ideas from that of hearing. (*Journal of Discourses*, 2:247)

> The spirit is inherently capable of experiencing the sensations of light; if it were not so, we could not see. You might form as fine an eye as ever was made, but if the spirit, in and of itself, were not capable of being acted upon by the rays of light, an eye would be of no benefit. Then unclothe the spirit; and instead of exposing a small portion of it about the size of a pea to the action of the rays of light, the whole of it would be exposed. I think we could then see in different directions at once, instead of looking in one particular direction, we could then look all around us at the same instant. (*Journal of Discourses*, 2:243)

This statement seems to me to be an extension of the doctrine taught in Doctrine and Covenants 88:67: "And if your eye be single to my glory, your whole bodies shall be filled with light, and there shall be no darkness in you; and that body which is filled with light comprehendeth all things."

Elder Pratt believed that the Spirit of God operating in the next life will have a more powerful and direct effect on the disembodied spirit of a person than it had upon the joined spirit and mortal body of that individual while in mortality:

> But when this Spirit of God, this great telescope that is used in the celestial heavens, is given to man, and he, through the aid of it, gazes upon eternal things, what does he behold? Not one object at a time, but a vast multitude of objects rush before his vision, and are present before his mind, filling him in a moment with the

knowledge of worlds more numerous than the sands of the sea shore. Will he be able to bear it? Yes, his mind is strengthened in proportion to the amount of information imparted. It is this tabernacle, in its present condition, that prevents us from a more enlarged understanding. . . . I believe we shall be freed, in the next world, in a great measure, from these narrow, contracted methods of thinking. Instead of thinking in one channel, and following up one certain course of reasoning to find a certain truth, knowledge will rush in from all quarters; it will come in like the light which flows from the sun, penetrating every part, informing the spirit, and giving understanding concerning ten thousand things at the same time; and the mind will be capable of receiving and retaining all. (*Journal of Discourses*, 2:246)

For Elder Pratt, as well as for many others possessing the gift of seership, the spirit world is a wonderful place. There we will be more awake, more alive, more sensitive to the powers of godliness than we ever were in this mortal sphere.

Thus, the great message of the death and resurrection of Jesus is twofold: first, the object of this life is more life; second, for those who try their best to keep the commandments, death is not a fearful event. We will still long to be reunited with our physical bodies, but the sting of death is eradicated through the incomprehensible power of the Lord Jesus Christ.

TEACHING THE SPIRITS

What joy, rejoicing, gladness, and gratitude greeted Jesus as he passed through the veil into paradise, there to extend his powers of mercy, redemption, and liberation to all who would receive them (D&C 138:15). When Jesus arrived in the spirit world, he commenced a unique work, something that had never been done before. President Brigham Young declared: "Jesus was the first man that ever went to preach to the spirits in prison, holding the keys of the Gospel of salvation to them. Those keys were delivered to him in the day and hour that he went into the spirit world, and with them he opened the door of salvation to the spirits in prison" (*Discourses of Brigham Young,* 378). Jesus is *the* Being in the universe who holds the keys of unlimited power over sin, death, hell, sorrow, suffering, the bottomless pit, the devil, and captivity (Revelation 1:18; 3:7; 9:1; 21:1–4).

This aspect of his ministry had long been foretold by Israel's ancient prophets. Isaiah spoke of it more than seven hundred years before it occurred: "The Spirit of the Lord God is upon me; because the Lord hath anointed me to preach good tidings unto the meek; he hath sent me to bind up the brokenhearted, to proclaim liberty to the captives, and the opening of the prison to them that are bound; to proclaim the acceptable year of the Lord, and the day of vengeance of our God; to comfort all that mourn" (Isaiah 61:1–2).

Jesus himself quoted this same prophecy at the beginning of his public ministry when he boldly proclaimed his messiahship in the little synagogue in his hometown of Nazareth. There he announced that the time had finally come for the preaching of the gospel to the living *and* the dead, that the spirits of the departed who had been confined in darkness in spirit prison would also be redeemed. They would go free from bondage upon accepting the Savior's gospel.

The Savior's visit to the spirit world and the commencement of his unique work among the dead involved as much delegation of authority as did his ministry in mortality. In one of the greatest revelations of this dispensation, President Joseph F. Smith saw for himself that Jesus Christ confined his visit to paradise and that, as holder of the keys of the work for the dead, he commissioned and organized the faithful spirits in paradise to visit the other spirits of the unbaptized, unrighteous, ungodly, unrepentant, disobedient, rebellious, and ignorant in order to proclaim liberty to them by teaching the gospel of Jesus Christ. Wrote President Smith:

> And as I wondered, my eyes were opened, and my understanding quickened, and I perceived that the Lord went not in person among the wicked and the disobedient who had rejected the truth, to teach them;
>
> But behold, from among the righteous, he organized his forces and appointed messengers, clothed with power and authority, and commissioned them to go forth and carry the light of the gospel to them that were in darkness, even to all the spirits of men; and thus was the gospel preached to the dead.
>
> And the chosen messengers went forth to declare the acceptable day of the Lord and proclaim liberty to the captives who were bound, even unto all who would repent of their sins and receive the gospel.
>
> Thus was the gospel preached to those who had died in their sins, without a knowledge of the truth, or in transgression, having rejected the prophets.
>
> These were taught faith in God, repentance from sin, vicarious baptism for the remission of sins, the gift of the Holy Ghost by the laying on of hands,
>
> And all other principles of the gospel that were necessary for them to know in order to qualify themselves that

they might be judged according to men in the flesh, but live according to God in the spirit. (D&C 138:29–34)

PRIESTHOOD IN THE SPIRIT WORLD

As the Savior passed through the veil, he was met by such noble and great leaders in mortality as Adam and Eve—the parents of all mortals—and Abel, Seth, Noah, Shem, Abraham, Isaac, Jacob, Moses, Isaiah, Ezekiel, Daniel, Elias, Malachi, all the prophets who dwelt among the Nephites, and many, many more (D&C 138:38–49). These formed part of the missionary force organized to teach the gospel to those in spirit prison. They were delegated keys of power and authority to do so by the Savior. Just as none in mortality are sanctioned to go forth to preach the gospel or build up the Church without authorization (D&C 42:11), so none in the spirit world were sent forth without being given authority. Note again the language of President Smith's vision: "But behold, from among the righteous, he organized his forces and appointed messengers, clothed with power and authority, and commissioned them to go forth and carry the light of the gospel to them that were in darkness, even to all the spirits of men; and thus was the gospel preached to the dead" (D&C 138:30).

Such delegation by the Lord Jesus Christ implies the continuing operation of the priesthood in the world of spirits. "As in earth, so in the spirit world," declared Elder Parley P. Pratt. "No person can enter into the privileges of the Gospel, until the keys are turned, and the Gospel opened by those in authority" (*Journal of Discourses*, 1:11). Of the authorized ministers in the spirit world, President Joseph F. Smith further said, "They are there, having carried with them from here the holy Priesthood that they received under authority, and which was conferred upon them in the flesh" (*Gospel Doctrine*, 471–72). President Brigham Young observed that "when a person passes behind the vail, he can only officiate in the spirit world; but when he is resurrected he officiates as a resurrected being, and not as a mortal being" (*Journal of Discourses*, 9:89).

The Savior's work among the righteous dead in the spirit world, and his act of delegating authority to them so they could help others there, enlarges our picture of the operation of the priesthood in time and eternity. Truly, the priesthood is eternal. Its existence spans premortality, mortality, and the postmortal world. The Prophet Joseph Smith declared, "The Priesthood is an everlasting principle, and existed with God from eternity, and will to eternity, without beginning of days or end of years" (*Teachings of the Prophet Joseph Smith*, 157). Moreover, modern prophets have declared that righteous men did indeed hold the priesthood in our premortal existence. President Joseph Fielding Smith presents us with this insightful declaration: "With regard to the holding of the priesthood in the preexistence, I will say that there was an organization there just as well as an organization here, and men there held authority. Men chosen to positions of trust in the spirit world held the priesthood" (Conference Report, October 1966, 84).

The foregoing is consistent with President Joseph F. Smith's panoramic vision and perspective, which also spanned premortality and the postmortal spirit world. Speaking of the missionaries and ministers of the gospel in the spirit world, he said: "I observed that they were also among the noble and great ones who were chosen in the beginning to be rulers in the Church of God. Even before they were born, they, with many others, received their first lessons in the world of spirits and were prepared to come forth in the due time of the Lord to labor in his vineyard for the salvation of the souls of men" (D&C 138:55–56). President Joseph F. Smith also saw that the missionary work begun in the spirit world at the time Jesus inaugurated the spirit-prison mission continues in our own day by "the faithful elders of this dispensation" who have passed on (D&C 138:57).

Memories of my own father come flooding back to my mind when I read this portion of President Smith's vision. My father was a seventy and a stake missionary at the time he passed away, a real force for missionary work in the area where we lived. Even at a young age I could tell he felt genuine passion for the work and for his quorum. Members of that quorum helped bury my father. Members of that quorum helped comfort my family. Members of that quorum helped send me on a full-time mission, and I love them as my father did. My father's regular Sunday assignment was teaching a special Gospel Doctrine class to inmates at the nearby federal prison. I know he cherished that opportunity. I have thought since, and I believe it is so, that he is now teaching prisoners of a different kind.

Priesthood holders are not the only ones involved in this work among the dead. President Smith offered this truly profound and important insight about sisters involved in the work of salvation in the spirit world:

> Now, among all these millions of spirits that have lived on the earth and have passed away, from generation to generation, since the beginning of the world, without the knowledge of the gospel—among them you may count that at least one-half are women. Who is going to preach the gospel to the women? Who is going

to carry the testimony of Jesus Christ to the hearts of the women who have passed away without a knowledge of the gospel? Well, to my mind, it is a simple thing. These good sisters who have been set apart, ordained to the work, called to it, authorized by the authority of the holy Priesthood to minister for their sex, in the House of God for the living and for the dead, will be fully authorized and empowered to preach the gospel and minister to the women while the elders and prophets are preaching it to the men. The things we experience here are typical of the things of God and the life beyond us. There is a great similarity between God's purposes as manifested here and his purposes as carried out in his presence and kingdom. Those who are authorized to preach the gospel here and are appointed here to do that work will not be idle after they have passed away, but will continue to exercise the rights that they obtained here under the Priesthood of the Son of God to minister for the salvation of those who have died without a knowledge of the truth. (*Gospel Doctrine,* 461)

Just as sisters in this life are called and authorized to preach the gospel in the earth, often working among other women, so sisters in the next life are called and authorized to be messengers of the Lord's gospel, ministering specifically among women. It will be remembered that President Smith made it a point of stating explicitly in his vision of the spirit world that he saw "our glorious Mother Eve, with many of her faithful daughters who had lived through the ages and worshiped the true and living God" (D&C 138:39). It is to be assumed that these were part of the Savior's "forces and appointed messengers, clothed with power and authority, and commissioned . . . to go forth and carry the light of the gospel to them that were in darkness" (D&C 138:30). In addition, it should be remembered that sisters are delegated specific authority, under priesthood direction, to minister to women who enter the Lord's house to receive temple ordinances.

ANOTHER PHASE OF THE ATONEMENT COMPLETED

Truly, the gospel is for all of our Heavenly Father's children—"black and white, bond and free, male and female; and he remembereth the heathen; and all are alike unto God" (2 Nephi 26:33). In no place or way do we see with greater clarity the fulfillment of this scripture than in the Savior's continuing ministry to the spirit world. The chief apostle in the meridian dispensation, Peter, confirmed Nephi's statement about God's all-inclusive love and fairness when he explained how the Atonement applies to both the living and the dead and why Jesus went to the spirit world after his mortal mission was finished: "For Christ also hath once suffered for sins, the just for the unjust, that he might bring us to God, being put to death in the flesh, but quickened by the Spirit: by which also he went and preached unto the spirits in prison. . . . For for this cause was the gospel preached also to them that are dead, that they might be judged according to men in the flesh, but live according to God in the spirit" (1 Peter 3:18–19; 4:6).

These verses are quite remarkable. Many in the Christian community cannot fully explain them. But as Latter-day Saints, we can imagine quite easily what powerful visions of the spirit world Peter was privileged to see that enabled him to teach this doctrine so succinctly and with such power. His experience must have been akin to Joseph F. Smith's manifestation as recorded in Doctrine and Covenants 138. Though no canonical record of Peter's own manifestations have survived, the distillations and conclusions of such manifestations have been preserved, both in the writings of Peter as well as Paul.

Before the coming of Jesus to the world of spirits, those spirits could not be judged according to men in the flesh while living according to God in the Spirit because the gospel had not ever been preached to the dead. The great gulf had not been bridged. Baptisms for the dead had not been performed. "Not until Christ had organized his missionary forces in the world of spirits do we find references to the Saints practicing the ordinance of baptism for the dead (1 Corinthians 15:29)" (Millet and McConkie, *Life Beyond*, 51). Jesus' visit to the spirit world changed the universe forever. Those "dead who had been confined in darkness *not knowing their fate*" could be set free (Smith, *Answers to Gospel Questions*, 2:81; emphasis added).

With the great gulf in the spirit world finally bridged after thousands of years of waiting on the part of all those who had died from Adam to Christ, Jesus was prepared to fulfill the next phase of the glorious and infinite atonement. President Howard W. Hunter called this phase "the single most fundamental and crucial doctrine in the Christian religion," the one thing that "cannot be overemphasized, nor . . . disregarded," and "the ultimate triumph" as well as "the ultimate miracle" (Conference Report, April 1986, 18). This, of course, is the literal, physical, bodily, resurrection of Jesus of Nazareth.

But now is Christ risen from the dead, and become the firstfruits of them that slept.

For since by man came death, by man came also the resurrection of the dead.

For as in Adam all die, even so in Christ shall all be made alive.

But every man in his own order: Christ the firstfruits; afterward they that are Christ's at his coming.

1 CORINTHIANS 15:20–23

CHAPTER 4

Firstfruits of the Resurrection

To bring to pass the resurrection, Jesus left the spirit world and went back to the dark, sealed tomb where his lifeless physical body had been interred since Friday. It was very early Sunday morning, at sunrise (Mark 16:2).

The scriptural record is silent regarding the moments just before and just after the Savior reentered his physical body to become an incorruptible, living "soul" (the spirit *and* the body compose the soul; D&C 88:15). We possess accounts of what death is like from those who have actually passed through the veil, but we have no reliable records of what it is like for a spirit to reenter his or her physical body and become a resurrected being. Yet, from the truth that to be without one's physical body is a bondage and a period of anxious waiting for the resurrection, we deduce that the time of the reuniting of spirit and body is a moment of great joy, exultation, and wonderment. We also believe that when the Savior of all humankind left the spirit world to take up his physical body, every spirit in paradise and many in spirit prison felt the same joy, gladness, and rejoicing as when he first arrived in the spirit world (D&C 138:15) and that they bowed the knee in acknowledgment and appreciation of Jesus' absolute power over death (D&C 138:23).

Jesus' departure from the world of spirits signaled the long-awaited actual opening of the prison doors. The righteous spirits knew that after the Savior's resurrection they too would be able to leave the spirit world and take up their own physical bodies forever. They would go free! It must have been a moment of jubilation in the spirit world as well as in the heavenly courts when the Savior's spirit departed for his body in the Garden Tomb.

Jesus himself had many ancestors and family members in the spirit world when he went there. His illustrious mortal genealogy is listed in the Gospels of Matthew (chapter 1) and Luke (chapter 3). Included are the names of kings and prophets in ancient Israel whom Jesus undoubtedly visited personally during his sojourn in the spirit world—Adam, Abraham, Jacob, Jesse, Hezekiah, Josiah, and many, many more. While Matthew's genealogy is generally regarded as the kingly list (the list of legitimate successors to the Davidic throne), Luke's is regarded as the father-to-son genealogy and hence the Savior's ancestry on Mary's side. It is particularly illuminating and satisfying to note that of the four women named in Matthew's genealogical list, three are gentile converts to the covenant (Tamar, Rahab, and Ruth), thus teaching us in subtle ways that there are *no* second-class citizens in the kingdom of God and that the Son of God himself descended from "converts."

All these were in the world of spirits. They were there when the greatest of all their descendants prepared to leave the realm of spirits and take up his physical body again. And among them there was great joy and exultation over the Savior's ultimate victory over sin and death, members of his own extended mortal family praising the name of him who was their actual great- . . . grandson, as well as the literal son of Elohim. (God and mortal man were thus linked through the birth of Jesus.)

Watershed events in our eternal journey, events marking the passage from one phase of our eternal existence to the next, are sacred moments. The birth of a child and the death of a loved one are such events, and many of us have felt the sanctity of these occasions. A close friend related to me how he was with his mother when she passed through the veil. With profound emotion he said that even though it was hard to see her go, it was a sacred experience. Surely, the passage from the spirit world to the resurrected state is such an occasion, and this was no less true for Jesus than for any of us. It also seems true that while the actual moments of these sacred occurrences (birth and death specifically) are private, the commemorations surrounding them often involve many people. Perhaps some living in our day were privileged to participate in the celebration of the Savior's resurrection, even though they would have been unembodied premortal spirits at the time, not disembodied postmortal spirits. After all, the hosts of heaven, some of which are undoubtedly living today, were privileged to participate in the heavenly celebration of the Savior's birth into mortality, which the Gospel of Luke chronicles (Luke 2:13–14).

The scriptures impress us with the thought that there are no mortal words sufficient to express what the Savior's resurrection meant to those in the spirit world, as well as countless unborn spirits. In fact, when we contemplate the magnitude of what the Savior accomplished as he left the spirit world and reentered his physical body, which had been lying in the Garden Tomb since his crucifixion, we marvel at the awesome power held uniquely by Jesus of Nazareth. Of all who have lived or will live on the earth, Jesus stands alone in his genetic makeup and powers. He is "the only one who possessed life in himself and power over death inherently. Christ was never subject unto death, even on the cross, but death was ever subject unto him" (Smith, *Doctrines of Salvation,* 1:31).

We do not know what it was like for the Savior, who in one moment had been a conscious, thinking entity in the spirit world and in the next moment was opening his eyes, clothed again in a physical body. Would it have been similar to awakening from sleep? We do not know. What we do know is that Jesus had that experience and, because of him, so will every other person who has ever lived on the earth (Alma 11:41). But the scriptures do not record the details of the resurrection itself.

It is significant that the most dramatic and remarkable moment in the history of Creation—the resurrection of Jesus Christ—is not described by any authoritative sacred text. This is perhaps witness enough that the actual moment of resurrection is intensely sacred and private. "This is one of the most remarkable things about the Gospel accounts of those strange early morning events. Not one of them actually describes Jesus' resurrection! This is the great event which the women (and eventually others) concluded must have taken place before their arrival at the tomb. This is the great event on which the rest of the New Testament entirely depends. It can be deduced by reflecting on the subsequent appearances of Jesus to his disciples (how could he be seen, if he had not first been raised?), but in itself it is never described" (Walker, *Weekend That Changed the World,* 46).

The reluctance of the Gospel writers to describe the details of the resurrection adds to their credibility rather than detracts from it. They wrote what they knew and what they were inspired to communicate. They were not in the spirit world when the Savior departed to go back to the sepulchre, nor were they in the tomb at the moment of resurrection. Either Jesus did not tell them what had happened or they were constrained by the Spirit not to write what they had learned. Some details of sacred events are not for public knowledge, as the Savior's prayers and interactions with his American Israelites show us (3 Nephi 17:15; 19:32). More than a hundred years after the Gospels were written an apocryphal work entitled the Gospel of Peter attempted to fill in the gaps and satisfy the readers' "need to know." But in the end, reading such things turns out to be a spiritually unfulfilling and unsatisfying experience, whereas the power of the canonical Gospels continues to draw us back to the Lord's atonement.

FIRSTFRUITS

Jesus was the firstfruits of the resurrection, meaning he was the first living thing of all Creation to be resurrected. He was the "firstfruits of them that slept" (1 Corinthians 15:20). When Jesus' spirit reentered his physical body in the Garden Tomb that first resurrection morning, he became the first person on this earth to take up again an immortal physical body, nevermore to die. Our English word *resurrection* derives from two Latin terms, *re* ("again") and *surgere* ("to rise"), and literally means "to rise again." Furthermore, the Latin *surgere* is the basis of our English word *surge* and conveys a sense of power. Jesus' rising again was accomplished with power.

Jesus inherited the power to choose when to lay down his life and the power to take it up again from his literal Father, Elohim. He testified of this fact on at least two occasions during his mortal ministry (John 5:26; 10:17–18). Genetically, he had life in himself. In this regard, as well as in other significant aspects, he was different from all human beings who ever have or ever will live on this earth or the millions like it in the universe. And this godly power, in association with his sinless life and substitutionary payment for our sins by the shedding of his blood, is the power by which all others will be resurrected. President Joseph Fielding Smith affirmed this doctrine:

> Now, we have not power to lay down our lives and take them again. But Jesus had power to lay down his life, and he had power to take it up again, and when he was put to death on the cross, he yielded to those wicked Jews. When he was nailed to the cross, he meekly submitted, but he had power within himself, and he could have resisted. He came into the world to die that we might live, and *his atonement for sin and death is the force by which we are raised to immortality and eternal life.* (*Doctrines of Salvation,* 1:128; emphasis added)

Elder Bruce R. McConkie also taught that "because of his [Jesus'] resurrection, 'by the power of God,' all men shall come forth from the grave. (Morm. 9:13.)" (*Mormon Doctrine,* 639).

The power of Christ's atonement and resurrection is so great, so profound, that all people will be resurrected. Whether or not they have been righteous makes no difference. Whether or not they want to be resurrected makes no difference. The resurrection is inevitable—all who have lived in mortality will be resurrected. The apostle Paul's sure witness is still one of the clearest: "For since by man came death, by man came also the resurrection of the dead. For as in Adam all die, even so in Christ shall all be made alive. But every man in his own order:

Christ the firstfruits; afterward they that are Christ's at his coming" (1 Corinthians 15:21–23).

While the certainty of a universal resurrection for human
beings may be well known, the applicability of the universal resurrection to all created things possessing a spirit may not be so
well known. But so far-reaching is the power of the Savior's
Atonement that it extends to this earth as well as to the creatures living on it. President Joseph Fielding Smith taught that
"the Lord intends to save not only the earth and the heavens,
not only man who dwells upon the earth, but all things which he
has created. The animals, the fishes of the sea, the fowls of the
air, as well as man, are to be recreated, or renewed, through the
resurrection, for they too are living souls. The earth, as a living
body, will have to die and be resurrected, for it, too, has been
redeemed by the blood of Jesus Christ" (*Doctrines of Salvation,*
1:74).

This teaching is in precise harmony with the revelations of
the Restoration. The Doctrine and Covenants provides a
poignant example:

> And again, verily, verily, I say unto you that when the
> thousand years are ended, and men again begin to deny
> their God, then will I spare the earth but for a little sea-
> son;
>
> And the end shall come, and the heaven and the
> earth shall be consumed and pass away, and there shall
> be a new heaven and a new earth.
>
> For all old things shall pass away, and all things shall
> become new, even the heaven and the earth, and all the
> fulness thereof, both men and beasts, the fowls of the air,
> and the fishes of the sea;

And not one hair, neither mote, shall be lost, for it is the workmanship of mine hand. (D&C 29:22–25)

The passing away of the earth and its becoming new are simply another way of saying that the earth will be resurrected to a celestial condition and become the abode of celestial beings. "This earth is living and must die, but since it keeps the law it shall be restored through the resurrection by which it shall become celestialized and the abode of celestial beings" (Smith, *Doctrines of Salvation*, 1:73; see also D&C 130:9). The reference to neither hair nor mote being lost is precise language used by the Lord in this revelation to convey the idea of the infinite restorative power of the resurrection (see also Alma 40:19–23).

Still more stunning is the truth that not only this earth but also the millions of earths like this one will be resurrected by the infinite power of Jesus Christ. In explaining this doctrine, President Joseph Fielding Smith acknowledged that this earth, on which we now dwell, is destined for a celestial resurrection. Then he said:

> Other earths, no doubt, are being prepared as habitations for terrestrial and telestial beings, for there must be places prepared for those who fail to obtain celestial glory, who receive immortality but not eternal life. Moreover, since the Lord has never created anything to be destroyed, every earth, whether created for celestial glory, or for terrestrial or telestial, will have to pass through the condition of death and the resurrection, just the same as our earth will have to do. The "passing away," therefore, means that after they have finished their "probationary state" in mortality, they will die and be raised again to receive the "glory" for which they were

designed, and to become the eternal abodes of man. (*Doctrines of Salvation*, 1:72–73)

The ramifications of Jesus' resurrection are not just staggering but truly incomprehensible to our finite minds. His greatness is towering, his power is limitless, and yet his love for each individual, for you and for me, is private and personal. On the one hand, he can send a planet hurtling through space, and yet, on the other hand, know the name and innermost thoughts of every one of his followers. No wonder we ought to remember him always (D&C 20:77, 79); we ought to worship him and our Father from the depths of our soul every day; we ought to have a prayer in our hearts continually (Alma 34:18–27). Even then we can scarcely begin to comprehend him, or his power, or the magnitude of what happened in the Garden Tomb that first Easter Sunday morning.

KEYS OF RESURRECTION

Those who have spoken authoritatively about the resurrection have sometimes spoken of it as an ordinance involving keys, the same way other priesthood ordinances require the operation of priesthood power and priesthood keys. President Brigham Young has given us profound and insightful commentary on the core doctrine of the Christian faith:

All who have lived on the earth according to the best light they had, and would have received the fulness of the Gospel had it been preached to them, are worthy of a glorious resurrection, and will attain to this by being administered for, in the flesh, by those who have the authority. All others will have a resurrection, and receive a glory, except those who have sinned against the Holy

89

Ghost. It is supposed by this people that we have all the ordinances in our possession for life and salvation, and exaltation, and that we are administering in these ordinances. This is not the case. We are in possession of all the ordinances that can be administered in the flesh; but there are other ordinances and administrations that must be administered beyond this world. I know you would ask what they are. I will mention one. We have not, neither can we receive here, the ordinance and the keys of the resurrection. They will be given to those who have passed off this stage of action and have received their bodies again, as many have already done and many more will. They will be ordained by those who hold the keys of the resurrection, to go forth and resurrect the Saints, just as we receive the ordinance of baptism, then the keys of authority to baptize others for the remission of their sins. This is one of the ordinances we cannot receive here, and there are many more. We hold the authority to dispose of, alter and change the elements; but we have not received authority to organize native element, to even make a spear of grass grow. (*Discourses of Brigham Young,* 397–98)

Closer to our day, President Spencer W. Kimball, in a general conference address in April 1977, confirmed that no one now living holds the keys of resurrection. And that is *not* because we lack the desire to possess them. President Kimball said: "Do we have the keys of resurrection? . . . I buried my mother when I was eleven, my father when I was in my early twenties. I have missed my parents much. If I had the power of resurrection as did the Savior of the world, I would have been tempted to try to have

90

kept them longer. . . . We do not know of anyone who can resurrect the dead as did Jesus the Christ when he came back to mortality" (Conference Report, April 1977, 69).

Nevertheless, President Kimball promised, the faithful will receive not only the keys of resurrection but also the power of godhood in the resurrection: "We talk about the gospel in its fulness; yet we realize that a large part is still available to us as we prepare, as we perfect, and as we become more like our God. In the Doctrine and Covenants we read of Abraham, who has already attained godhood. He has received many powers, undoubtedly, that we would like to have and will eventually get if we continue faithful and perfect our lives" (Conference Report, April 1977, 71).

When Jesus' spirit reentered his physical body in the Garden Tomb that first Easter morning, he became the first person on this earth to receive the keys of resurrection. It is true that he inherited *the power* to take up his body again from his Father (Elohim) at the time of his mortal birth. But he received *the keys* of resurrection only after his own resurrection. President Joseph Fielding Smith explained the sequence this way: "Jesus Christ did for us something that we could not do for ourselves, through his infinite atonement. On the third day after the crucifixion he took up his body and *gained the keys of the resurrection,* and thus has power to open the graves for all men, but this he could not do until he had first passed through death himself and conquered" (*Doctrines of Salvation,* 1:128; emphasis added).

This is important doctrine, for it means that the keys of resurrection are conferred *after* one has been resurrected and those keys are then used to resurrect others. Jesus was the prototype. Having obtained the keys of resurrection himself (after his own experience with resurrection), he then possessed power to resurrect all others. According to President Brigham Young, those keys of resurrection first acquired by the Savior are then further given, extended, or delegated to others who have died and been resurrected. "They will be ordained, by those who hold the keys of the resurrection, to go forth and resurrect the Saints, just as we receive the ordinance of baptism, then the keys of authority to baptize others" (*Discourses of Brigham Young*, 398).

Thus, in one respect we might think of the ordinance of resurrection as being like other ordinances which we see performed on this earth. It involves those who possess the authority and keys of resurrection. As President Brigham Young and Elder Erastus Snow also taught, the resurrection will be conducted much as other things are done in the kingdom, by delegation (*Journal of Discourses*, 6:275; 15:136–39; 25:34). Just as we cannot bless or baptize ourselves, so we cannot resurrect ourselves. Ordinances are performed on our behalf by those who are authorized to perform the ordinances.

Knowing what we do about the importance of worthy fathers guiding and blessing their families in righteousness, it does not seem out of order to believe that worthy fathers and priesthood holders will have the privilege of calling forth their wives, or their children, or even other members of their family from the grave. Is it not the order of heaven for righteous patriarchs (fathers, grandfathers, and others) to bless, baptize, and perform other ordinances for their loved ones?

Before Jesus was resurrected, only his Father, our Father in Heaven, possessed the keys of resurrection (even though as the Son of God he possessed the power of life in himself—independently). After he was resurrected, Jesus acquired the keys of resurrection which could then be given to others.

The illuminating statements of President Young, President

Kimball, and President Smith, taken together, help us to see once again that God's house is a house of order. As a result of his own resurrection, Jesus now controls all power and all keys, under the direction of his Father, which he delegates to others as they are worthy and become prepared to possess the various powers of godliness. These powers are then used to bless the human family. This is true for the keys of resurrection as well as all other power and authority.

LEAVING THE TOMB BEHIND

Early in the morning on that first Easter Sunday, when Jesus took up his physical body again in the Garden Tomb, where it had been placed the previous Friday, the entire universe, all of creation, every earth in the cosmos, every living thing, were changed for eternity. We do not know the details of the actual resurrection process or what went on inside the Garden Tomb immediately after the resurrection. We do not know how long Jesus was there. We *do* know that Jesus passed through his burial clothes, leaving them lying in place, in the outline and form of the body around which they had been wrapped. Resurrected bodies have the power to move through solid objects. John records in his own Gospel that when he came to the tomb and looked inside and when Peter entered it shortly thereafter, they both saw the strips of burial linen lying in place in the burial chamber as well as the burial cloth that had been wrapped around Jesus' head (John 20:4–7). The strips of cloth "were left in such a way as to show that his resurrected body had passed through their folds and strands without the need of unwinding the strips or untying the napkin" (McConkie, *Mortal Messiah*, 4:268).

This was explicit evidence of Jesus' resurrection. No mortal man had disturbed his body. The cloth that had been wrapped about Jesus' head ("napkin" in the King James Version) was still by itself, separate from the linen, just as it had been before the resurrection. The Greek word used in John 20:7, *entetuligmenon* (literally, "having been wrapped up"), has sometimes been translated as "folded," presumably because translators have not understood the power a resurrected body has over the elements and solid objects.

Jesus, then, left his burial clothing in place as one more witness of the greatest of the miraculous acts that compose the Atonement. The scriptures make no mention of Jesus donning postresurrection robes or clothing, but such was surely the case.

Thus, we know very little of the details regarding what happened inside the Garden Tomb on resurrection morning. Outside the tomb, however, momentous events were unfolding. These events are described in varying degrees of completeness by the four Gospels. At some point early in the morning there was a violent earthquake. Two angels of the Lord descended from heaven and rolled back the great stone from the door of the tomb (JST Matthew 28:2). The guards on watch were so afraid at the sight of the angels that they shook uncontrollably and became like dead men—meaning that they collapsed on the ground (Matthew 28:2–4; Mark 16:3–4; Luke 24:2; John 20:1). One scholar has pointed out an early Christian tradition that identified the angels as Michael and Gabriel (Matthews, "Resurrection," 317). Perhaps this is true. Surely, the angelic messengers were not chosen randomly. Michael is Adam, the Father of the human family that included Jesus. Adam introduced mortality through the Fall, which condition Jesus atoned for. Gabriel is Noah. He stands next in authority to Adam and announced the births of Jesus and John the Baptist (Luke 1:11–37; Smith, *Teachings of the Prophet Joseph Smith*, 157).

The guards, who had been commissioned to keep watch at Jesus' tomb and who thought they acted in the strength of Roman and Jewish support, were now helpless. All their military might was powerless. Days earlier, Jesus had declined the assistance of angels when he was arrested by a lynch mob at the entrance to the garden of Gethsemane (Matthew 26:53–54). Now, he did not mind at all their presence at the Garden Tomb (Keller, *Rabboni*, 289). Their presence was incontrovertible evidence that God was in charge there.

Once the guards had sufficiently recovered from their fright, they fled from the place in terror, even though Roman military law decreed death as the penalty for soldiers deserting their posts (Talmage, *Jesus the Christ*, 678). Matthew is ambiguous concerning when the tomb was opened, but the other Gospels make it clear that this happened before the women arrived at the tomb to complete their preparations of Jesus' body in anticipation of a long interment.

Jesus did not need angels to roll away the great stone from the door of the sepulchre so that he could leave. Resurrected beings have power to pass through the elements and objects of the earth, as we have seen with Jesus' burial clothing. In the resurrection we shall become acquainted with a whole other dimension of the laws of physics. President Joseph Fielding Smith taught:

> Resurrected bodies pass through solid objects. Resurrected bodies have control over the elements. How do you think the bodies will get out of the graves at the resurrection? When the Angel Moroni appeared to the

Prophet Joseph Smith, the Prophet saw him apparently come down and ascend through the solid walls, or ceiling of the building. If the Prophet's account had been a fraud, he never would have stated such a story . . . but would have had the angel come in through the door. Why should it appear any more impossible for a resurrected being to pass through solid objects than for a spirit, for a spirit is also matter?

It was just as easy for the Angel Moroni to come to the Prophet Joseph Smith down through the building as it was for our Savior to appear to his disciples after his resurrection in the room where they were assembled when the door was closed. . . .

How could he do it? He had power over the elements. (*Doctrines of Salvation*, 2:288)

Why, then, did the angels roll the stone away and open the tomb? First, there was undoubtedly important symbolic meaning in this act. Just as the door of the Garden Tomb was now open, signaling its Occupant was no longer there, so too the door of spirit prison was now open, signaling that its righteous inhabitants were free and would no longer be confined there. This is not unlike the tearing of the veil of the Jerusalem Temple at the moment of the Crucifixion. The exposed Holy of Holies symbolized, among other things, a new order or dispensation that allowed, through the atonement of Christ, all the righteous to enter the presence of God—which the Holy of Holies represented (Hebrews 9:19–24; 10:19–20).

Second, with the opening of the tomb, the disciples could look inside as well as enter the sepulchre and know for themselves that the tomb was empty, that Jesus had come back to life, that he really was the Messiah! And that is exactly the effect the empty tomb and the discarded burial clothes had on the disciples when they had the opportunity to peer inside, as John poignantly describes: "Then went in [to the Garden Tomb] also that other disciple [in addition to Peter], which came first to the sepulchre, and he saw, *and believed*" (John 20:8; emphasis added). We know from internal evidence in the Gospel of John that "the other disciple" was John himself. Sometimes he also referred to himself in his Gospel account as the "disciple whom Jesus loved" (John 13:23; 19:26; 20:2; 21:7, 20).

Others would likewise come to the tomb, and out of their initial experience with its emptiness would eventually blossom the witness that Jesus was who he said he was, that he had told the truth, that he was the Savior, Messiah, and Son of God alive again!

But Mary stood without at the sepulchre weeping: and as she wept, she stooped down, and looked into the sepulchre,

And seeth two angels in white sitting, the one at the head, and the other at the feet, where the body of Jesus had lain.

And they say unto her, Woman, why weepest thou? She saith unto them, Because they have taken away my Lord, and I know not where they have laid him.

And when she had thus said, she turned herself back, and saw Jesus standing, and knew not that it was Jesus.

Jesus saith unto her, Woman, why weepest thou? whom seekest thou? She, supposing him to be the gardener, saith unto him, Sir, if thou have borne him hence, tell me where thou hast laid him, and I will take him away.

Jesus saith unto her, Mary. She turned herself, and saith unto him, Rabboni; which is to say, Master.

JOHN 20:11–16

CHAPTER 5

First Witnesses of His Resurrection

T here is general agreement among the synoptic Gospels that it was very early on Sunday morning, at dawn, the first day of the week, when Mary Magdalene and the other women (including Mary, mother of James, and Salome) went back to the Garden Tomb (Matthew 28:1; Mark 16:2; Luke 24:1). John adds the detail that it was still dark (John 20:1). Their main purpose in going to the tomb so early was to anoint the body of Jesus, to complete the unfinished business of final burial preparations of the corpse (Mark 16:1; Luke 24:1). There may have also been another reason for the visit as well, which is hinted at by Matthew when he states that they came "to see the sepulchre" (Matthew 28:1).

According to Jewish custom, a visit to the tomb of a deceased person within three days after interment was required in order to check the condition of the corpse. This obligation is outlined in the Mishnah, *Tractate Semahot* 8:1: "One should go to the cemetery to check the dead within three days, and not fear that such [an action] smacks of pagan practices. There was actually one buried man who was visited after three days and lived for twenty-five more years and had sons, and died afterward" (quoted in Kloner, "Did a Rolling Stone Close Jesus' Tomb?" 76).

Presumably, Jesus' disciples did not go to the tomb expecting to find the Master revived, for they had witnessed for themselves the horrible effects of the crucifixion process. It is possible, however, and perhaps even probable, that they also visited the tomb within three days to fulfill the custom of the Jews—the oral tradition. (We know these disciples were exacting in keeping other parts of the Law.) Also important to note is that their counting of burial days followed Jewish custom, which included both the day of burial and the next two days (any portion of the third day) in the count (Kloner, "Did a Rolling Stone Close Jesus' Tomb?" 29). Thus, the resurrection of Jesus of Nazareth, King of the Jews, on "the third day" (Matthew 16:21) accorded with Jewish custom and practice.

WOMEN FIND THE TOMB OPEN

As the women entered the garden area and approached the tomb in the early-dawn darkness, surely there must have been a somber, even grief-stricken, mood among them. As they carried their spices and preparations, they naturally wondered out loud how they would get the heavy, cumbersome stone rolled away from the entrance of the sepulchre (Mark 16:3). So preoccupied with grief and plans for final burial preparations had they been that they had not thought of this little detail.

Much to their surprise, and perhaps apprehension, when they arrived at the tomb they found the "very great" stone already rolled away. From John's comment we realize that Mary Magdalene certainly was not thinking in terms of resurrection, though resurrection was part of the Jewish belief system of that time. Rather, upon seeing the opened tomb Mary Magdalene immediately left the other women and ran to find Peter and John, two of the three chief apostles of the Church, to alert them that mischief was afoot: "They have taken away the Lord out of the sepulchre, and *we* know not where they have laid him" (John 20:2; emphasis added). Her worst fears were now realized. Even in death her Master, their Master, could not be allowed to rest in peace. John does not tell us who Mary suspected of tampering with Jesus' body, but both the Jewish conspirators and the Roman crucifiers would have been possibilities.

Because John's account of Sunday morning does not mention the other women named in the synoptic Gospels, some have reasoned that Mary Magdalene was alone and not in the company of these other women when she first went to the tomb. Yet, we note her use of the pronoun *we* in her description of surprise at discovering the tomb already open. Perhaps she was the one who ran back to find Peter and John because hers was a more immediate sense of loss at seeing no corpse in the tomb.

ANGELS AT THE TOMB

Though it is not made explicitly clear how the exact sequence of events unfolded next, especially when we read the four Gospel accounts together, it is more than likely that Matthew, Mark, and Luke describe details of the story involving the rest of the women left back at the tomb, while John recounts the details of Mary Magdalene's departure to notify Peter and John.

As the other women drew near to the opened sepulchre for the first time that morning, they saw two angels, not one as reported in the King James Version of Matthew and Mark. The angels were dressed in long, white, shining (glorious) garments

(JST Matthew 28:2; JST Mark 16:3; JST Luke 24:2). Matthew adds that their countenance was like lightning and their raiment was as white as snow (JST Matthew 28:3). The Joseph Smith Translation is a tremendous gift in helping to clarify our understanding of events that first resurrection morning. Even that inspired document, however, preserves some of the disagreements between the individual Gospel accounts regarding details. For example, Mark and Luke do not agree about whether the angels were sitting on or standing by the great stone. But such things are of lesser importance.

Mark next reports that to assuage the fear of the women upon seeing two heavenly beings (and certainly also to build their faith in the resurrection), the angels declared the monumental, universal, culminating message of the Atonement: "Be not affrighted; ye seek Jesus of Nazareth, who was crucified; he is risen; he is not here; behold the place where they laid him; and go your way, tell his disciples and Peter, that he goeth before you into Galilee; there shall ye see him as he said unto you. And they, entering into the sepulcher, saw the place where they laid Jesus" (JST Mark 16:4–6). It is striking that Peter is mentioned separate and apart from the other disciples. There is no question that the Gospel authors regard him as the leader of the group. In fact, he is usually singled out in texts that discuss the disciples.

Luke describes a slightly different order in the sequence of events when the women encountered the angels. He notes that they experienced both perplexity and fear but that those feelings surfaced *after* they entered the tomb and saw there was no body: "And they found the stone rolled away from the sepulcher, and two angels standing by it in shining garments. And they entered into the sepulcher, and not finding the body of the Lord Jesus, they were much perplexed thereabout; and were affrighted, and bowed down their faces to the earth. But behold the angels said unto them, Why seek ye the living among the dead?" (JST Luke 24:2–4).

Though real, the differences in the testimonies of the synoptic Gospels regarding details of the women's experience at the tomb are understandable. The authors were different individuals, writing from their own perspectives based on personal knowledge or remembrances of the events, or, in the case of Luke and perhaps Mark, reflecting what eyewitnesses had told them. The fact that not even the Joseph Smith Translation attempts to harmonize the accounts indicates to me that the authors were not in collusion, not making up a story, nor repeating a popular legend. I am persuaded that the Prophet Joseph Smith was inspired to simply restore what each of the authors had originally written. The Joseph Smith Translation is preserving original text here because that is what the Lord wanted us to have. The Gospel writers were not infallible nor flawless. They may have seen things differently or understood things differently. But they were authentic witnesses. What is impressive in the Joseph Smith Translation is the emphasis in all three synoptic Gospels on the appearance of two angels, not one, and, thus, the fulfillment of the ancient law of witnesses to establish the certainty of the event (Deuteronomy 19:15; 2 Corinthians 13:1). The angels constituted a powerful and sure witness that the resurrection of Jesus Christ really did happen.

All of us have had great teachers. The greatest teachers help us to know what teachings are most important; they help us to order our thoughts by emphasizing what is critical and turning our minds to significant connections with past information. The two angelic witnesses did this very thing for the women at the tomb by recalling the Savior's own testimony of his inevitable resurrection given on an earlier occasion. After asking the women why they were seeking the living among the dead, the angels then declared: "He is not here, but is risen: remember how he spake unto you when he was yet in Galilee, saying, The Son of man must be delivered into the hands of sinful men, and be crucified, and the third day rise again. And they remembered his words" (Luke 24:6–8).

As a result of this divine instruction, the women began to understand. They began to gain a testimony of the Savior's resurrection. That testimony would become complete and made sure a little while later when the living Lord himself appeared to them personally. In the meantime, the women had also been instructed to go quickly and tell the other disciples what they had just learned—that Jesus "is risen from the dead; and, behold, he goeth before you into Galilee: there shall ye see him" (Matthew 28:7; Mark 16:7). A testimony is strengthened in the bearing of it.

In a wonderfully poignant description of their reaction to all that they had just experienced in the last several minutes at the tomb, Matthew says of the women, "And they departed quickly from the sepulchre with *fear* and *great joy;* and did run to bring his disciples word" (Matthew 28:8; emphasis added). There was no dallying. They had been told the Master was alive, and their errand was pressing. They did depart quickly, so much so that they *ran* to tell the others what they had just seen and heard. They were filled with both joy and fear.

Though there are many ways to interpret the word "fear," its use here in tandem with the phrase "great joy" seems to intend something like excitement mingled with a feeling of anxiety. Mark's Gospel says of the women, "They trembled and were amazed" (Mark 16:8). In moments such as the one just described, single words or phrases are often inadequate to convey the range of emotions that we feel. "Anyone in similar circumstances would have been startled out of their minds—and these were aging women after an emotionally draining weekend, now caught unawares in a dim, damp tomb at dawn" (Walker, *Weekend That Changed the World*, 48). Sometimes we experience fear over things we do not understand. Sometimes we become anxious over our own worthiness or status before the Lord. Doubtless the women did not comprehend all that was happening, but they knew they had experienced something colossal.

APOSTLES RECEIVE THE NEWS

Luke reports that the women who had been instructed by the angels returned from the tomb, located the eleven living members of the Quorum of the Twelve, and rehearsed their experience to them as well as "to all the rest," meaning the other disciples who were staying in close contact with the apostles (Luke 24:9). Luke also reveals the identity of the women who were now in the presence of the apostles explaining their encounter with the empty tomb and the angels. They were Mary Magdalene, Joanna, Mary the mother of James, and the other women who were with them (Luke 24:10). We do not know how many of these "other women" there were, but it may have been several, and we know of their long-time devotion to Jesus (Luke 8:2–3).

That Luke includes Mary Magdalene in his list is puzzling at first glance when, as we have seen, John implies that Mary left the group of women upon first seeing the stone rolled away from the tomb. If we regard Mary Magdalene as having been with the rest of the women the whole time—that is, from the beginning of their experience with the two angels—then we face the

105

challenge of explaining the language and tone of Mary's speech reported in John 20:2: "They have taken away the Lord . . . and we know not where they have *laid* him" (emphasis added). These words imply that Mary had not heard the testimony of the angels, that she did not know about Jesus' coming back to life, and that she believed the corpse had simply been laid somewhere else by someone of unknown identity.

It seems to me that Mary Magdalene was included in Luke's list for two reasons. First, she was originally with the women who approached the tomb during the early hours of that Sunday morning, and Luke was aware of who was in the group of women that first went to the tomb. Second, Mary Magdalene was reunited with the rest of the women when they also arrived to talk to Peter, John, and the others to report their experience with the angels. By that time Mary Magdalene had already spoken with the apostles and explained her fear and consternation over the disappearance of Jesus' body. So all the women who started out together for the Garden Tomb ended up together at the abode of the apostles. Luke may not have known about Mary's separate appeal to the apostles, or knowing about it, he may not have written down the details exactly as we would have wished.

I do not believe that Mary Magdalene would have maintained a posture or tone of disbelief over the idea of Jesus' resurrection (as is portrayed in John 20:2) if she had been privileged to hear the powerful testimony of the two angelic sentinels at the tomb. We must remember that when the other women heard the angels recount Jesus' own words about his eventual resurrection, "they remembered his words" (Luke 24:8). Mary's speech as reported by John does not sound like she yet remembered anything about the Savior's predictions of his resurrection. Furthermore, if Mary Magdalene had been privy to the powerful witness of the angels at the tomb, along with the other women, we would expect her to have more readily recognized the identity of the Savior when he appeared to her in the garden. But instead, she seems to possess no sense of forewarning that her Master could have been resurrected; there is no hint of anticipation when it comes to the declaration of the angels, "He is risen."

Not only did Mary Magdalene not yet believe in the resurrection of Jesus but the apostles also dismissed the report of the other women regarding Jesus' resurrection. The words of the women "seemed to them as idle tales, and they [the apostles] believed them not" (Luke 24:11). In fact, we are inclined to think that Mary's previous comments about the body of Jesus being stolen away had prejudiced the apostles against the idea of Jesus being resurrected.

It was because of the reports by Mary and the other women that "Peter, therefore, went forth, and that other disciple, and came to the sepulchre" (John 20:3). As leaders of the band of Jesus' disciples, they undoubtedly felt the need to investigate the happenings at the tomb, if for no other reason than the fact that Mary's report conflicted with the report of the other women. Though they ran together, John was faster afoot and arrived at the sepulchre first, but did not enter. He reserved that honor for the senior and chief apostle, Peter. Elder Russell M. Nelson provided an important insight into this episode as it relates to the principle of seniority in the Quorum of the Twelve Apostles:

> Seniority is honored among ordained Apostles—
> even when entering or leaving a room. . . .
> Some [years] ago Elder Haight extended a special

courtesy to President Romney while they were in the upper room in the temple. President Romney was lingering behind for some reason, and [Elder Haight] did not want to precede him out the door. When President Romney signaled [for him] to go first, Elder Haight replied, "No, President, you go first."

President Romney replied with his humor, "What's the matter, David? Are you afraid I'm going to steal something?"

Such deference from a junior to a senior apostle is recorded in the New Testament. When Simon Peter and John the Beloved ran to investigate the report that the body of their crucified Lord had been taken from the sepulcher, John, being younger and swifter, arrived first, yet he did not enter. He deferred to the senior apostle, who entered the sepulcher first. (See John 20:2–6.) Seniority in the apostleship has long been a means by which the Lord selects His presiding high priest. (Conference Report, April 1993, 52)

Apparently, the angels had departed from the garden by the time Peter and John arrived, leaving the special witnesses alone to contemplate the meaning of the empty tomb and the burial clothing that had been left behind. In those sacred moments of reflection and inspiration, these amazing men gained a conviction of the reality of the resurrection of Jesus. "Upon John, reflective and mystic by nature, the reality dawns first. It is true! They had not known before; now they do" (McConkie, *Doctrinal New Testament Commentary*, 1:842).

They saw and felt and believed! Up to that point, they had not comprehended the meaning or import of the scripture "that he must rise again from the dead" (John 20:9; see also vv. 4–8). Now, possessing new light and fresh understanding, the chief apostle and his counselor "went away again unto their own home" as believers (John 20:10).

Some students of the New Testament have pointed out that Luke seems to contradict John's account by describing only Peter's visit to the empty tomb and omitting any mention of John's participation (Luke 24:12). Yet John was there, and Luke was not. John knew that both he and Peter had participated together in an extraordinary experience. In fact, Luke 24:12 is missing from some ancient manuscripts of the New Testament and may well be a later addition.

The two chief apostles did not need to see Jesus to believe in the resurrection, but they did need the Holy Spirit. The power of the Holy Ghost to reorder men's thinking, to change their beliefs, is limited only by the receptivity and spirituality of the individuals themselves. The power that the Holy Ghost has to change men and the universe is incomprehensible to our finite minds. This power includes the varied forces of nature—gravitation, sound, heat, light, electricity, nuclear forces—and other forces so far beyond our comprehension as to make what we know and understand, compared to what the Holy Ghost knows and understands, look like a packhorse compared to a locomotive (Talmage, *Articles of Faith*, 160–61).

The witness of the Holy Ghost is even greater and more important than a witness gained by experiencing visitations or seeing miracles. President Harold B. Lee said that he knew "that Jesus is the Christ, the Son of the Living God" by "a witness more powerful than sight" (*Ensign*, November 1971, 17). That witness came from the Holy Ghost, as President Joseph Fielding Smith declared: "The Lord has taught that there is a stronger witness than seeing a personage, even of seeing the Son of God in a vision. Impressions on the soul that come from the Holy Ghost are far more significant than a vision. When Spirit speaks to spirit, the imprint upon the soul is far more difficult to erase. Every member of the Church should have impressions that Jesus is the Son of God indelibly pictured on his soul through the witness of the Holy Ghost" ("First Presidency and the Council of the Twelve," November 1966, 979).

MARY MAGDALENE

During all that had transpired up to this point Sunday morning, no one had yet seen the risen Lord. That changed with Mary Magdalene, as Mark's terse comment proclaims: "Now when Jesus was risen early the first day of the week, he appeared *first* to Mary Magdalene" (Mark 16:9; emphasis added). Mary was the first mortal to whom Jesus showed himself as the resurrected Lord.

We do not know a great deal about Mary Magdalene from scriptural sources. More was written about her in postapostolic writings purporting to be scripture but which are part of the Apocrypha and Pseudepigrapha. And much more can be found in modern culture—both in print (fiction and nonfiction) as well as in movies. But none of these are canonical or even authoritative. We should not trust very much of what we hear or see written about Mary Magdalene outside of scripture. For example, there is a false tradition that equates Mary Magdalene with the unnamed sinner who washed the feet of Jesus with her tears and then anointed and wiped them with her hair (Luke 7:37–38). Perhaps the false identification arose, in part, because of the close proximity of this story in the last half of Luke 7 to the initial introduction of the name of Mary Magdalene in the first verses of Luke 8. But though the identification is wrong, it still continues to circulate (Talmage, *Jesus the Christ*, 263–64).

Mary (Hebrew, *Miriam*) was a very common name in first-century Judaism, and each was differentiated by some notable distinction. Mary Magdalene, or, better, Mary of Magdala, was denominated by her association with the small town of Magdala on the western shore of the Sea of Galilee. Many scholars identify it with the village known in the Talmud as Magdala Nunayya, or Magdala of the Fishes. The Aramaic name *Magdala* derives from the Hebrew *migdal*, meaning a "tower." The tower which gave this village its distinctive quality "was probably used to hang fish to dry in the sun and wind" (Murphy-O'Connor, "Fishers," 27). It would have been a place well known to Jesus and his apostles, who were fishermen on the Sea of Galilee.

Mary Magdalene was a woman of tremendous faith, charity, and action, as described in the Gospels. She was part of the group of women who traveled with Jesus and the Twelve from one town and village to another in the Galilee and who helped to support these brethren out of her own means (Luke 8:2–3). She had been healed by Jesus of demonic possession; out of her went seven devils, or evil spirits (Mark 16:9; Luke 8:2). It is likely that she, having remained with the Master throughout his ministry, was part of the group of women who watched and mourned as Jesus carried his cross to Golgotha and whom he specifically addressed when he turned and said, "Daughters of Jerusalem, weep not for me, but weep for yourselves, and for your children" (Luke 23:27–28). Mary Magdalene was at the cross during Jesus' crucifixion (Matthew 27:55–56; Mark 15:40–41; John 19:25). She was at the Garden Tomb during Jesus' burial (Matthew 27:61; Mark 15:47). And she was back at the Garden

Tomb early that Sunday morning with the other women (Matthew 28:1; Mark 16:1; Luke 24:10; John 20:1).

One other thing is certain. Like the other women from Galilee, Mary Magdalene was devoted to Jesus and the early Church of Jesus Christ. Elder James E. Talmage of the Quorum of the Twelve called Mary Magdalene a "noble woman" and "a devoted soul." She "became one of the closest friends Christ had among women; her devotion to Him as her Healer and as the One whom she adored as the Christ was unswerving; she stood close by the cross while other women tarried afar off in the time of His mortal agony; she was among the first at the sepulchre on the resurrection morning" (*Jesus the Christ*, 264–65). Therefore, it is not surprising to find Mary Magdalene back at the empty tomb, lingering for a while after Peter and John had seen the burial clothing and returned to their own homes as believers in the resurrection. "The sorrowful Magdalene had followed the two apostles back to the garden of the burial. No thought of the Lord's restoration to life appears to have found place in her grief-stricken heart; she knew only that the body of her beloved Master had disappeared" (*Jesus the Christ*, 680). She stayed, looking for answers, "because she had not seen the angels or heard their message . . . [She was] still uncertain and wondering at what [had] happened" (Mumford, *Harmony of the Gospels*, 163).

First Resurrection Appearance

John alone reports the powerful and touching scene that occurred as Mary, lingering alone with her thoughts, weeping from grief made doubly intense over the unknown whereabouts of the corpse of the Master she loved, full of tears at this final indignity and injustice, stooped down and looked into the tomb. There she saw two angels in white, sitting where the body of

Jesus had lain (John 20:12). From John's brief report, it appears that she did not recognize them as heavenly messengers, bearers of good tidings, perhaps because of her consuming grief. Her response to their tender inquiry about her tears was essentially the same she had given to Peter and John earlier that morning, "Because they have taken away my Lord, and I know not where they have laid him" (John 20:13).

Earlier, when Mary Magdalene talked with Peter and John, her statement was in the plural: "*We* know not where they have laid him." Now her response was in the singular. Before, she spoke for the whole group of women, expressing a sentiment whose essence was one of exasperation more than grief over the fulfillment of their suspicions that the body would not be left alone. Now Mary's expression was intensely personal and sorrowful. "The absence of the body, which she thought to be all that was left on earth of Him whom she loved so deeply, was a personal bereavement" (Talmage, *Jesus the Christ*, 680). As Elder Talmage further intimates, there is a volume of pathos, affliction, and affection in her words "They have taken away my Lord."

John makes no further mention of the angels, whose presence presaged the appearance of One greater. Turning away from the entrance to the empty tomb, Mary actually saw Jesus standing close by, but she did not know that it was he. It is not hard to understand why she would have mindlessly supposed that Jesus was the caretaker of the garden in which the tomb was located. It wasn't just that she was consumed by sorrow, although that was certainly overwhelming. It was also a matter of being desperate to find the body of her Master in order to spare him further indignities and prevent further disruptions of the Jewish customs for honorable burials, which, not inconsequentially, were regarded as carrying the force of Jewish law.

I have seen how important it is for faithful Orthodox Jews to observe their burial customs and how distraught they can become when those customs are in danger of being disrupted. On an airplane flight from the United States to the Holy Land, a group of Jews became panicky when the plane landed late and sundown was rapidly approaching, preventing them from properly observing burial customs for one of their great rabbinic leaders. The members of the traveling group were out of their seats and racing to the front of the plane as the aircraft was only beginning to taxi to the gate. As the flight attendants were trying to push them back to their seats and issuing stern commands over the intercom, one man kept saying, "You don't understand! You don't understand!" Similarly, perhaps, Mary's own grief and frustration prevented her from really "seeing" and comprehending reality.

When Jesus spoke to Mary, his was the first utterance of a resurrected being ever in history. He asked her the same thoughtful, sympathetic question that the angels had just put forward moments before: "Woman, why weepest thou? whom seekest thou?" Mary responded in a tone that indicates she presumed the gardener already knew something about the tomb's occupant because she did not mention Jesus' name. She referred to him only by the pronoun *him*. "Sir, if thou have borne *him* hence, tell me where thou hast laid *him*, and I will take *him* away" (John 20:15; emphasis added).

What happened next surely must rank among the most dramatic moments in human history. Uttering Mary's name as only he could, in an intonation that only she would recognize immediately, Jesus identified himself to the woman from Magdala. "Jesus saith unto her, Mary. She turned herself, and saith unto him, Rabboni; which is to say, Master" (John 20:16). We can only imagine the leap of Mary's heart as instantaneously the feelings of bewilderment and then recognition swept over her. "Who is this? Could it actually be—? Is he really alive after all I have seen happen? Yes, it really is Jesus—the Lord of life!"

Though scripture is silent regarding the exact thoughts and feelings of Mary at this moment of transcendent realization, Elder Talmage provides inspired commentary:

> One word from His living lips changed her agonized grief into ecstatic joy. . . . The voice, the tone, the tender accent she had heard and loved in the earlier days lifted her from the despairing depths into which she had sunk. She turned, and saw the Lord. In a transport of joy she reached our her arms to embrace Him, uttering only the endearing and worshipful word, "Rabboni," meaning My beloved Master. Jesus restrained her impulsive manifestation of reverent love, saying, "Touch me not; for I am not yet ascended to my father," and adding, "but go to my brethren, and say unto them, I ascend unto my Father, and your Father; and to my God, and your God." To a woman, to Mary of Magdala, was given the honor of being the first among mortals to behold a resurrected Soul, and that Soul, the Lord Jesus (Mark 16:9). (*Jesus the Christ*, 681)

As to why Mary was privileged to be the first mortal to see the risen Lord, the first Being ever to be resurrected, we are not told. For that matter, we are not told why all the women to whom the resurrected Savior first appeared were so blessed, but surely it had something to do with the way they cared for the Savior, giving all they had (economically, emotionally, materially, mentally) for him, in life and in death. There is no doubt that a special relationship existed between Jesus and Mary. But this part of the story of Christ's redeeming mission is noteworthy because of the way it highlights the relationship between the Savior and several women of the early Church. The women were the first to *see* the Lord—the first eyewitnesses of the resurrection. Elder Bruce R. McConkie wrote:

> How much there is incident to the death, burial, and resurrection of our Lord which ennobles and exalts faithful women. They wept at the cross, sought to care for his wounded and lifeless body, and came to his tomb to weep and worship for their friend and Master. And so it is not strange that we find a woman, Mary of Magdala, chosen and singled out from all the disciples, even including the apostles, to be the first mortal to see and bow in the presence of a resurrected being. Mary, who had been healed of much and who loved much, saw the risen Christ! (*Doctrinal New Testament Commentary,* 1:843)

It is interesting to me that Jesus does not, at this juncture, stop to give a discourse on the doctrine of resurrection. He does not stop to answer questions about the nature of his own experience. He does not stop to note the fulfillment of prophecies about this moment—either his own prophecies or those of other prophets. He does not ask that Mary or the others worship him. What he does do is refocus Mary's attention on God the Father. And he bids Mary do the same for others through her testimony. "Jesus saith unto her, Touch me not; for I am not yet ascended to my Father: but go to my brethren, and say unto them, I ascend unto my Father, and your Father; and to my God, and your God" (John 20:17).

The Savior's whole orientation, his life, his teaching focus, was always fixed on his Father, our Father in Heaven. It was *never* about himself, except as his role and position as the Only Begotten Son and Messiah related to his Father's plan, purposes, and desires. But here again we're back to the Father. This is an important model for us to follow. The best teacher, the best leader, the best parent, will always step out of the limelight and focus the attention of his or her students and family on the Father and the Son. In the most triumphant moment of his life, when Jesus had every right to proclaim his monumental victory over the great enemies of humankind—physical and spiritual death—the Redeemer of the universe quietly pointed Mary and the rest of us to his Father and his God, who is also our Father and our God.

John reports simply that Mary did as she had been instructed: "Mary Magdalene came and told the disciples that she had seen the Lord, and that he had spoken these things unto her" (John 20:18).

Entrenched ideas die hard. New notions are not easily accepted when they contradict previous experience. Such seems to have been the case with those disciples of the Lord whom Mary now tried to persuade that Jesus really had come back to life, that he was now a resurrected Personage. As Mark implies, their great grief seems to have kept them from believing Mary's eyewitness account: "And she went and told them that had been with him, as they mourned and wept. And they, when they had heard that he was alive, and had been seen of her, believed not" (Mark 16:10–11). It would take nothing less than the literal appearance of the Lord himself to change their sorrow into joy.

THE OTHER WOMEN

Absent from the group of unbelieving disciples at this juncture were the other women who had accompanied Mary

Magdalene to the Garden Tomb that early Sunday morning, and who had first heard the good news of Jesus' resurrection from angelic witnesses. To these women, the Lord appeared personally and confirmed their hopes and bolstered their believing hearts: "And as they went to tell his disciples, behold, Jesus met them, saying, All hail. And they came and held him by the feet, and worshipped him" (Matthew 28:9). They were given a personal audience with the Lord and felt the overwhelming desire to worship him. In this regard, Elder McConkie presents an interesting perspective:

> In his own infinite wisdom, Jesus chose to appear to and be handled by a group of other women—all before he came even to Peter and the rest of the Twelve. . . .
>
> These other women included Mary the mother of Joses; Joanna, evidently the wife of Chuza, Herod's steward (Luke 8:3); and Salome, the mother of James and John. Among them were women who had been with Jesus in Galilee. Certainly the beloved sisters from Bethany were there; and, in general, the group would have been made up of the same ones who have hovered in sorrow around the cross. Their total number may well have been in the dozens or scores. We know that women in general are more spiritual than men. . . .
>
> . . . But whoever they were, Jesus is using them and the fact of his resurrection to show the unity and oneness and equality of the man and the woman. (*Mortal Messiah*, 4:265–67)

To Mary Magdalene, Jesus forbade too-close physical contact, yet to these women he permitted their embrace of his feet. Why?

118

I believe four things are true. First, this was now a different Jesus, a different kind of Being from the one the disciples were used to associating with in mortality. He was now God resurrected. "There was about Him a divine dignity that forbade close personal familiarity" (Talmage, *Jesus the Christ*, 682).

Second, in John 20:17 Jesus was not actually forbidding Mary to "touch" him but rather forbidding her to hold on to or embrace him. In the Greek text of the English phrase, "Touch me not" (*me mou aptou*), the verb *aptou* means "to hold, to cling, or to fasten to." Jesus was saying, "Hold me not. Do not cling to me." Some translators even render this passage as, "Stop touching me." It seems only natural to me that Mary would be touching the Savior to confirm that she was not just seeing a mirage, but that he was a physical reality.

Third, as God resurrected, Jesus was now to be recognized as the successful agent of his Father's will, the One who had now fulfilled the Father's plan of salvation and had done *all* that the Father had asked of him. It was only fitting and proper that the Savior's first lengthy embrace be reserved for his literal Father, the God who loved him, empowered him, and sent him to earth (and whom the Savior loved in return with equal intensity). Thus, no one was permitted to cling to the Savior "until after He had presented Himself to the Father," who was deserving and desirous of that first postresurrection embrace (Talmage, *Jesus the Christ*, 682).

Fourth, when Mary spoke with her Lord, he had not yet been with his Father. She was the first to see him as a resurrected Being. Later, when he appeared to the other women, the Savior had already ascended to his Father and received his love and approbation. It is not difficult to imagine that Mary Magdalene would yet receive an embrace from her Lord.

The image presented by Matthew of the Savior greeting the women who had so affectionately cared for him in life and in death (Luke 8:2; 23:55–56; 24:1), and their response—embracing his feet and, no doubt, wetting those feet with their tears—is a particularly joyous and vibrant one. We do not know what words of comfort the Master spoke; however, the Greek word used by Matthew to indicate Jesus' greeting to the women (*chairete*) is translated as "All hail" in the King James Version. It derives from the Greek root *chairo*, meaning "to rejoice, be glad, be delighted." In other words, Matthew depicts a scene in which the risen Lord was as joyful at meeting and greeting the women as they were at meeting him. This is a profound moment captured in scripture.

The Book of Mormon preserves a similarly profound moment when disciples of the Savior worshiped at his feet at the time he first appeared to them on the American continent after his resurrection. Their response was the same as that of the women in the Old World: "And when they had all gone forth and witnessed for themselves, they did cry out with one accord, saying: Hosanna! Blessed be the name of the Most High God! And they did fall down at the feet of Jesus, and did worship him" (3 Nephi 11:16–17). Even though both groups of disciples knew that the Savior's love was personal and undemanding, their every instinct, impulse, and desire were to fall at his feet and worship the great God of the universe, so powerful was the force of his presence and personality.

The Sunday morning following Friday's crucifixion was the most important Sunday in history and a day of many firsts. It was the first time mortals had seen a resurrected being. It was the first time a resurrected being had spoken or been spoken to. It was the first time a resurrected body had been touched by mortal hands. It was the first time a Jewish Sabbath or holy day had been overshadowed by a regular week day. And now it was no longer a "regular" weekday. It would be memorialized forever as the day when the Lord God of Israel arose from the dead to bring life to all Creation for eternity. It was the first day that the first witnesses began to spread the news of the first resurrection—the ultimate act in the drama that is the Atonement.

For I delivered unto you first of all that which I also received, how that Christ died for our sins according to the scriptures;

And that he was buried, and that he rose again the third day according to the scriptures:

And that he was seen of Cephas, then of the twelve:

After that, he was seen of above five hundred brethren at once; of whom the greater part remain unto this present, but some are fallen asleep.

After that, he was seen of James; then of all the apostles.

And last of all he was seen of me also, as of one born out of due time.

1 Corinthians 15:3–8

CHAPTER 6

Other Sunday Witnesses

Though the first Easter morning had already been filled with momentous events, many more would occur before the day ended. We can hardly imagine a more stunning twenty-four hours. After the Savior's resurrection and his appearance to the group of first witnesses—the devoted women of the early Church—many ancient Saints were resurrected, and several more people saw the living Lord for themselves, including all but one of the members of the Quorum of the Twelve. These gained a personal assurance of the Savior's triumph over death.

THE FIRST RESURRECTION
AFTER CHRIST'S

In Matthew's record of the Crucifixion, which took place from 9 o'clock Friday morning to 3 o'clock Friday afternoon, is a brief notice telling us of others who were resurrected:

Jesus, when he had cried again with a loud voice, yielded up the ghost.

And, behold, the veil of the temple was rent in twain

from the top to the bottom; and the earth did quake, and the rocks rent;

And the graves were opened; and many bodies of the saints which slept arose,

And came out of the graves after his resurrection, and went into the holy city, and appeared unto many. (Matthew 27:50–53)

Though this report of additional resurrected beings is placed right after Jesus' death on the cross, it is unquestionably out of order chronologically from the sequence of events as they actually occurred on those fateful days—Friday through Sunday. We know with certainty that no living thing was resurrected before Jesus Christ, for he was "the firstfruits of them that slept" (1 Corinthians 15:20). Many individuals were resurrected after him, perhaps immediately after him on Sunday morning. But no person's resurrection preceded the Savior's.

Those who came forth from the grave and began appearing in Jerusalem's streets and byways after the Savior's resurrection were part of that group promised to come forth in the first resurrection. That this is actually the first resurrection spoken of in the scriptures is confirmed by Elder Bruce R. McConkie:

> To us the first resurrection shall commence when Christ comes again, and the second resurrection shall start at the end of the millennium. But for those who lived prior to the time of the resurrection of Christ, the first resurrection, itself a resurrection of the just, was the one which accompanied the coming forth of the Son of God from the grave. (*Doctrinal New Testament Commentary*, 1:847)

Several antemeridian prophets foretold this first resurrection years and even centuries before the birth of Jesus in Bethlehem. Enoch, Isaiah, and Samuel the Lamanite all spoke of others who would be resurrected when the Messiah took up his physical body again (Moses 7:55–56; Isaiah 26:19; Helaman 14:25; 3 Nephi 23:7–13). The clearest articulation of the doctrine of the first resurrection that would occur at the time of Christ's rising from the dead was given by the prophet Abinadi in the American hemisphere 148 years before the birth of Christ. Abinadi declared:

> And there cometh a resurrection, even a first resurrection; yea, even a resurrection of those that have been, and who are, and who shall be, even until the resurrection of Christ—for so shall he be called.
>
> And now, the resurrection of all the prophets, and all those that have believed in their words, or all those that have kept the commandments of God, shall come forth in the first resurrection; therefore, they are the first resurrection.
>
> They are raised to dwell with God who has redeemed them; thus they have eternal life through Christ, who has broken the bands of death.
>
> And these are those who have part in the first resurrection; and these are they that have died before Christ came, in their ignorance, not having salvation declared unto them. And thus the Lord bringeth about the restoration of these; and they have a part in the first resurrection, or have eternal life, being redeemed by the Lord. (Mosiah 15:21–24)

That which Abinadi prophesied came to pass, as Matthew's

record certifies. At least two other things about Abinadi's prophecy are also impressive. First, he spoke as one who had already witnessed Christ's resurrection (in the past tense), even though he was living some seventeen decades *before* it actually happened. As he said, eternal life comes "through Christ, who *has broken* the bands of death" (Mosiah 15:23; emphasis added). Abinadi operated in the "prophetic future"—his witness was sure and certain. True prophecy is history in reverse.

Second, Abinadi delineated who it was that would be privileged to participate in the first resurrection. He mentioned specifically the prophets, the followers of the prophets, and those who kept the commandments—in short, the righteous, the Saints in ancient times who lived in the Old and in the New World. He also briefly mentioned a curious category of individuals who "died before Christ came" but who died "in their ignorance, not having salvation declared unto them" (Mosiah 15:24).

Upon reflection we realize that Abinadi's description is in harmony with a revelation received by the Prophet Joseph Smith wherein he saw the celestial kingdom of God and the inhabitants of that kingdom, including his father, mother, and brother Alvin. The Prophet marveled over how Alvin had obtained such an inheritance when he had died before the restoration of the gospel occurred and therefore had not been baptized for the remission of sins, which is the entryway to the celestial kingdom. The Lord's response to Joseph's wonderment applies not only to those who have died in this dispensation without hearing the fulness of the gospel of Jesus Christ preached, but also to those who died prior to the first coming of Christ without having been able to hear the gospel of Jesus Christ preached. The Prophet recorded:

Thus came the voice of the Lord unto me, saying: All who have died without a knowledge of this gospel, who would have received it if they had been permitted to tarry, shall be heirs of the celestial kingdom of God;

Also all that shall die henceforth without a knowledge of it, who would have received it with all their hearts, shall be heirs of that kingdom;

For I, the Lord, will judge all men according to their works, according to the desire of their hearts. (D&C 137:7–9)

This is one of the most heartening scriptural texts ever recorded in regard to the infinite mercy and fairness of God. As Alvin Smith's circumstances testify, only a relatively small percentage of our Heavenly Father's children will have the opportunity to hear and understand the fulness of the gospel of Jesus Christ while living in mortality. But each and every individual will be given a fair and equal chance at some point to hear, understand, and embrace the great plan of happiness, according to the word of the Lord revealed through the Prophet Joseph Smith. How different this message is from the false or uninformed beliefs of some others, who either do not know what will become of those who died before hearing the saving truths of Christ's eternal gospel, or who believe that those who died before hearing the message of salvation through Jesus Christ are lost forever.

Doctrine and Covenants 137 is also one of the most important scriptural passages ever revealed in helping us to understand the unique and incomparable competence of Jesus Christ to preside as the ultimate Judge. Only he and the Father know the desires and intents of our individual hearts (D&C 6:16). Thus, only he and the Father were in a position to determine who could participate in that first resurrection spoken of by Abinadi and reported by Matthew the apostle.

In the end, all judgment has been delegated to Jesus by the Father (John 5:22). For this we can be eternally grateful. After all, Jesus is not a leader who is immune to, or cannot be moved by, our infirmities. Neither is he partial or unfair in his judgment. Rather, he is perfectly empathetic and perfectly fair. He was tempted and tried and made to suffer like us. And because he experienced personally the greatest injustice ever perpetrated on any being in mortality, he desires (and knows how to bring about) perfect justice, fairness, and equity for each of us. Therefore, we may come boldly to him in time of need and find mercy and help sufficient for any problem or challenge we face (Hebrews 4:15–16).

Because only Jesus and his Father can know every extenuating circumstance of our individual lives and therefore render perfectly fair judgment, we mortals *must* refrain from judging unrighteously. I am reminded of my obligation and opportunity to cultivate a charitable attitude toward others when I think of the Lord's carefully orchestrated plan for all of his children, as described by Elder Ezra Taft Benson:

> God, the Father of us all, uses the men of the earth, especially good men, to accomplish his purposes. It has been true in the past, it is true today, it will be true in the future.
>
> "Perhaps the Lord needs such men on the outside of His Church to help it along," said the late Elder Orson F. Whitney of the Quorum of the Twelve. "They are among its auxiliaries, and can do more good for the cause where

the Lord has placed them, than anywhere else. . . . Hence, some are drawn into the fold and receive a testimony of the truth; while others remain unconverted . . . the beauties and glories of the gospel being veiled temporarily from their view, for a wise purpose. The Lord will open their eyes in His own due time. God is using more than one people for the accomplishment of His great and marvelous work. The Latter-day Saints cannot do it all. It is too vast, too arduous for any one people. . . . We have no quarrel with the Gentiles. They are our partners in a certain sense" (*Conference Report,* April 1928, p. 59). ("Civic Standards," 59)

Practically speaking, this means that I must not become depressed or irritated if others, especially friends or loved ones, do not join the Church or do not always see things the way I do. There may be a wise purpose in it, and a higher power may be operating. Heavenly Father is in charge, and he will care for his children. He loved them long before I did. My obligation and opportunity is to be tolerant and kind to everyone and to show gratitude for the talents and contributions of others.

RESURRECTED WITNESSES

The resurrected persons who came forth from their graves after Jesus' resurrection and appeared unto many living in the city of Jerusalem constituted another mighty and unimpeachable assembly of witnesses testifying to the reality of the resurrection of Jesus Christ, as well as to the certainty of a universal resurrection for all humankind. They had just come from the same spirit world where Jesus had sojourned. They had seen him

129

there and witnessed his ministry to the hosts of disembodied spirits. They exulted in his power to open the doors of their prison. They undoubtedly rejoiced when he left the spirit world to take up his physical body again, and they were still rejoicing at the time of their own resurrection and rescue from the bondage of death and the chains of hell. They knew that all they had experienced in terms of redemption was made possible by the resurrection of the Redeemer, the Son of God, the Prince of Life.

To whom these resurrected Saints appeared, and for how long, we do not know. Matthew does not expound upon his brief description, but knowing what we do about the significance of families in the Father's plan, we should not be surprised if we were to learn that these newly resurrected prophets and righteous Saints of ancient Israel appeared to their descendants as well as to those needing a boost to their faith in those troubled times. We can only imagine the shock or even consternation that the "many" people in Jerusalem must have experienced on that day of resurrection as they saw those who had been dead come back to life.

Whether or not these resurrected persons were able to influence others to believe in Jesus as the Messiah, the scriptures do not say. Perhaps. But sacred history teaches us that even the appearance of angels does not always have a lasting effect on people either to convert them or to motivate them to change their ways. It did not do much for two of father Lehi's sons, Laman and Lemuel (1 Nephi 3:29; 17:45).

After these newly resurrected beings finished their visit among Jerusalem's inhabitants, we assume they left this earth and took up residence in the presence of God as described by the Prophet Joseph Smith: "The angels do not reside on a planet like this earth; but they reside in the presence of God, on a globe like a sea of glass and fire, where all things for their glory are manifest, past, present, and future, and are continually before the Lord. The place where God resides is a great Urim and Thummim" (D&C 130:6–8).

Here the term *angel* is to be understood as meaning a resurrected being (Smith, *Teachings of the Prophet Joseph Smith*, 191). These resurrected personages not only had the privilege of dwelling in the Father's presence, but also of being further taught and ministered to by Jesus Christ himself. The Prophet Joseph taught that "Jesus Christ went in body after His resurrection, to minister to resurrected bodies" (*Teachings of the Prophet Joseph Smith*, 191). The only resurrected bodies to minister to were those who had arisen from the grave after the resurrection of the Lord Jesus Christ.

Of these souls who were resurrected after the Lord, Elder Parley P. Pratt wrote: "When Jesus Christ had returned from his mission in the spirit world, had triumphed over the grave, and had reentered his fleshly tabernacle, then the Saints who had obeyed the gospel while in the flesh and had slept in death or finished their sojourn in the spirit world were called forth to reenter their bodies and *to ascend with him to mansions and thrones of eternal power,* while the residue of the spirits remained in the world of spirits to await another call" (*Key to the Science of Theology*, 82; emphasis added).

Nevertheless, the resurrected righteous will not always dwell on a planet apart from this earth. In a future day this earth itself will be sanctified and transformed into a celestial sphere. It too will be taken "back into the presence of God" as a resurrected entity and be "crowned with celestial glory." It will become the permanent abode of those who once dwelled upon it in mortality, and who were subsequently resurrected and inherited the celestial kingdom (Smith, *Teachings of the Prophet Joseph Smith*, 191; D&C 88:16–20; 130:9). This is the ultimate purpose for which this earth was made. The ultimate destiny of the righteous is to inherit the celestial kingdom and dwell on this earth forever—with our loved ones in a state of glory and true happiness.

Although the scriptures are clear that a universal resurrection is guaranteed and that the ancient Saints mentioned in Matthew's Gospel constituted the vanguard of that all-encompassing resurrection, it is not clear how many have been resurrected since the first century. President Ezra Taft Benson, thirteenth president of The Church of Jesus Christ of Latter-day Saints, taught that the idea of a continuous resurrection since the time of the Savior's resurrection "is not scripturally true." He continued:

> But we do know that it is possible for our Father to call from the graves those whom He needs to perform special missions and special service. For example, we know of at least three who have been called up since the resurrection of the Master and since that first mass resurrection when the graves were opened and many of the Saints arose.
>
> Peter and James who came and laid their hands upon the Prophet Joseph and ordained him to the Melchizedek Priesthood were resurrected beings who lived and ministered after the time that the Master was upon the earth. Moroni, who lived and died many years after the time of the resurrection of the Master, was a resurrected being. So we know that there are some that

have been resurrected, and we know that certain promises are made that if the Lord needs the help of certain special messengers they may be called up. We are trying to live so that we will be worthy to come forth in the morning of this resurrection that will come preceding the great millennial period. The righteous will be caught up to meet the Savior as He comes in glory and makes His second appearance to rule and reign here in the earth when the millennial period will begin. (*Teachings of Ezra Taft Benson*, 18)

From President Benson we learn that though some individuals have been resurrected since the Savior's day, there has not been a constant, on-going resurrection of souls up to the present, involving very many of the Lord's righteous followers. The resurrection of the just is yet future and will take place at the second coming of Christ.

THE CONSPIRACY CONTINUED

As the ramifications of the empty tomb were becoming increasingly clear, and the number of witnesses to the reality of the resurrection continued to grow, a separate minidrama, of sorts, unfolded inside the city and involved the Roman soldiers who had fled their watch at the Garden Tomb earlier that Sunday morning. Matthew, who reports the event, does not tell us where the scene took place, although we imagine the palace of the high priest as a likely setting. Matthew was the only Gospel writer who told of the initial posting of guards at the tomb (Matthew 27:62–66), and he follows up his earlier account by describing the soldiers' report of their experiences at the tomb (Matthew 28:11–15).

At the same time the women set out on their way to spread the good news of the Savior's resurrection, having been commissioned to do so by the risen Lord moments before, the soldiers were in the city seeking out the chief priests to explain what had happened to them. They were unnerved, unwitting witnesses of God's awesome work. It was now useless for them to return to and stand beside an empty tomb.

The chief priests heard the soldiers and then met with the elders of the people to devise a plan that included bribing the soldiers with a large sum of money in return for their commitment to perpetuate a false report. The chief priests instructed the soldiers: "You are to say, 'His disciples came during the night and stole him away while we were asleep.'" The chief priests guaranteed the soldiers that if their report of this whole business got back to the Roman governor, they (the chief priests and Jewish leaders) would satisfy the governor and keep the soldiers out of trouble (Matthew 28:12–14).

Matthew concludes his account of this great deception by adding poignantly: "So they [the soldiers] took the money, and did as they were taught: and this saying is commonly reported among the Jews until this day" (Matthew 28:15). It must have been a huge sum of money offered to the soldiers, or tremendous pressure put on them, or both. Admitting to falling asleep while on guard duty could have serious consequences for them, even resulting in their execution. Even more amazing is the story the soldiers were supposed to uphold. Upon mature reflection, it becomes downright ridiculous. How could the soldiers know the body of Jesus had been stolen by his disciples if they were asleep?

But the chief priests were desperate to make the whole situation surrounding Jesus go away. They had manipulated his trial, railroaded him into a conviction, and then all but forced the Roman governor to administer the death penalty. Now the hapless soldiers appeared before them, subtly bearing testimony that Jesus really was who he said he was and had indeed risen from the dead. Undoubtedly, this unnerved these Jewish leaders. Therefore, they fell back to that course of action which came so naturally to them in dealing with the case of Jesus of Nazareth—manipulation and deception.

Matthew notes that the false story of the soldiers continued to be perpetuated among the Jewish people up to the time that he was writing his Gospel (he uses the phrase "to this day"). Sadly, the story continued to be promulgated long after Matthew's day. "Justin Martyr's Dialogue with Trypho (ch. 108) shows that the same calumny was current in the middle of the second century" (*Interpreter's Bible*, 7:620). In fact, it continued to circulate among certain groups of Jewish people for centuries. The great and learned biographer of Jesus Christ, Frederic Farrar, notes that the false story "continued to be received among them [certain Jewish groups] for centuries, and is one of the . . . follies repeated and amplified twelve centuries afterwards in the *Toldoth Jeshu*," a book discussing Jesus (*Life of Christ*, 644).

Thus, the legacy of the chief priests' original deception may have been to keep generations of good people from coming to a true understanding and knowledge of their Redeemer. The proclamation of the reality of the resurrection and redemption wrought by Jesus was intended for all humankind. A knowledge of this rescue from sin, death, sorrow, and suffering can lift in times of despair, empower in times of weakness, strengthen in times of sorrow. It is saddening to think that even a few might have been kept from this knowledge because of past leaders. It would seem the chief priests of that period have much to answer for. They hurt their own people—the people of Israel.

ON THE ROAD TO EMMAUS

After his appearances to Mary Magdalene and the other faithful women of the kingdom, Jesus began confirming his living presence to others, including the chief apostle Peter and two male disciples on the road to Emmaus.

"That Jesus did appear to Peter we know; that this appearance came after that to Mary Magdala, and after that to the other women, we also know—thus making it, as we suppose, his third appearance. But we do not know where or under what circumstances he came, or what words of comfort and counsel and direction he gave. In the upper room, with Peter present, the apostolic witness was borne: 'The Lord is risen indeed, and hath appeared to Simon'; and Paul says, 'he was seen of Cephas, then of the twelve' (1 Cor. 15:5)" (McConkie, *Mortal Messiah,* 4:272).

As Elder McConkie indicates, we know nothing about the setting of Peter's encounter with his risen Master (Luke 24:34), but surely it was a time in which the chief apostle's tears (over his denial of knowing Jesus two days earlier) were dried by the only One who could dry them. Peter was healed emotionally. Perhaps the scriptures are silent about this meeting because "it was an event too sacred and personal to be made a matter for public knowledge" (Walker, *Weekend That Changed the World,* 53).

The next two disciples to know of Jesus' resurrection received their witness in a most dramatic fashion. "It [was] the afternoon of the day of his resurrection" (McConkie, *Mortal Messiah,* 4:275). According to Luke, the two had left Jerusalem that Resurrection Sunday on their way to the village of Emmaus. It was after they had been told by the women who were at the sepulchre early that morning that Jesus was risen from the dead. Piecing things together, we know that this was the report that the women disciples had given to Peter and the others after they encountered the angels at the empty tomb but before they were actually visited by the resurrected Lord himself (Luke 24:9–11, 22–24; Matthew 28:9–10). By their own admission, the report of the women had caused the two travelers to Emmaus some genuine astonishment over, but apparently not acceptance of, the idea that Jesus could possibly be alive again (Luke 24:22).

In fact, the tone of the comments of the disciples on the road to Emmaus betrays their feelings of utter disappointment, sadness, and grief. "We trusted that it *had been* he [note the past tense] which should have redeemed Israel," they said. But, "the chief priests and our rulers delivered him . . . and have crucified him" (Luke 24:20–21; emphasis added). In other words, they were saying they had put their trust in Jesus but that trust was destroyed when he was executed. To them Jesus didn't look very messianic when hanging on the cross. The true Messiah, in their minds, was to be full of power to save, yet Jesus was not, or did not appear to be, empowered to do anything to save himself, let alone others. "And beside all this," they added, "today is the third day since these things were done" (Luke 24:21). This was an obvious reference to Jesus' promises that he would rise again on the third day (Matthew 16:21). They were aware of the promise, but it was the third day and they had not seen any evidence of his resurrection, only heard the wishful comments of emotional women.

As the two brethren walked down the road to the village of

Emmaus, which many scholars believe to have been located at or near the modern village of Moza (three and one-half miles northwest of Jerusalem), naturally they could think and speak about only one matter—"all these things which had happened" in Jerusalem the last three days. A stranger approached. It was Jesus, though they did not recognize him because "their eyes were holden that they should not know him" (Luke 24:16).

Several factors may have contributed to the disciples' lack of recognition. First, Jesus withheld his glory from the two disciples, which is something resurrected beings are capable of doing (Smith, *Teachings of the Prophet Joseph Smith,* 325; Pratt, *Key to the Science of Theology,* 70, 72). Second, the disciples were not expecting Jesus to be resurrected, let alone to appear to them personally on a dusty road outside Jerusalem. Third, as most travelers did, Jesus may have covered his head with a cloak to keep off the sun and the dust as he walked along. This would have partially sheltered his face from the disciples' view. Fourth, the disciples may have been so sad or consumed with grief that they didn't much care about the specific identity of who it was that joined them. He was just another Passover pilgrim as far as they were concerned.

In fact, Jesus spoke to the disciples as though he were just another stranger: "What manner of communications are these that ye have one to another as ye walk, and are sad?" (Luke 24:17). This question is evidence that the disciples' gloom was palpable. Speaking for both of them, Cleopas's response betrayed their incredulity and perhaps even irritation: "Art thou only a stranger in Jerusalem, and hast not known the things which are come to pass there in these days?" Jesus simply asked, "What things?" (Luke 24:18–19).

The disciples went on to explain what had transpired the past three days, including the report of the women that very morning about angels and an empty tomb. Apparently, Cleopas and his unnamed traveling companion had not yet heard of Mary Magdalene's personal experience. They walked along, possessed of that special misery born of lack of hope in the redemption of Christ.

In a remarkable response, Jesus chastised the disciples for their lack of belief as well as limited spiritual understanding. "Then he said unto them, O fools, and slow of heart to believe all that the prophets have spoken: Ought not Christ to have suffered these things, and to enter into his glory? And beginning at Moses and all the prophets, he expounded unto them in all the scriptures the things concerning himself. And they drew nigh unto the village, whither they went: and he made as though he would have gone further" (Luke 24:25–28).

The effect of Jesus' teaching on the disciples was profound and may have taken a rather lengthy period of time, perhaps several hours. For as they approached the village, the disciples asked Jesus to stay with them since it was "toward evening, and the day [was] far spent" (Luke 24:29). He accepted their invitation, and as he sat to eat with them—taking the bread, breaking it and blessing it in familiar fashion—the eyes of the disciples were opened, "and they knew him." The veil that had prevented them from recognizing him vanished. The posture of his body, the way the words of the blessing were pronounced, the expression of the face, and, not inconsequentially, the way the hands moved—the hands that still bore the wounds of crucifixion—all contributed to the disciples' epiphany. I can imagine the shock the two disciples experienced when they saw the hands and wrists of their supposed stranger. This was the

Master! At that moment they too came to know for themselves that all that had been said about Jesus' resurrection was absolutely, unequivocally true. And then he vanished from their sight (Luke 24:29–31).

Many are the lessons to be gleaned from the experience of the disciples on the road to Emmaus. First, sadness, when wallowed in, can sometimes prevent even good people from seeing the obvious. Second, like the ancient disciples, when we modern disciples are "slow of heart to believe all that the prophets have spoken," we are fools. Third, Moses and all the prophets in the Old Testament had the witness of the Messiah as their ultimate message. In fact, as Jesus shows us by his method of scriptural explication to the two disciples, the Old Testament truly was and is the human family's first treatment of Jesus Christ. Fourth, just as the Savior used the scriptures to teach of his divinity, so should all of us. Fifth, Jesus used just the right teaching method that fit the circumstances and created the setting which suited his pedagogical purposes. He did not attempt to deceive the disciples, but he did use their lack of recognition to draw out of them the information he needed to best teach them. This serves as an example for all teachers. Sixth, Jesus also kept his identity hidden from the disciples in order to demonstrate the nature of a resurrected body. "Our Lord had a purpose over and above that of interpreting the Messianic word. . . . His mission was to show them what a resurrected person is like" (McConkie, *Mortal Messiah*, 4:277).

Luke concluded his report of the experience of the two disciples in a most significant way, perhaps because he had experienced personally the same kind of confirming witness of Jesus' divinity and resurrection. He helps us to see that *what* Jesus said

140

to the disciples was important, but how they *felt* when he said it was of greater value in affirming their conviction of his godly stature. After Jesus left, "they said one to another, Did not our heart burn within us, while he talked with us by the way, and while he opened to us the scriptures?" (Luke 24:32).

It is worth repeating that the witness of the Holy Ghost is the greatest conviction we may receive. The Holy Ghost operates under the direction of Jesus Christ (John 16:13–14). The Holy Ghost is commissioned to bear witness of the Father and the Son (2 Nephi 31:18). The Holy Ghost causes our hearts to burn within us (3 Nephi 11:3; D&C 9:8). The Holy Ghost is one of the Lord's greatest gifts to his disciples in any age or dispensation, but it is likely one of the most underused gifts we have ever received.

Now possessing a sure witness of the divinity and resurrection of Christ, the disciples could not wait to return to Jerusalem that very hour and add their testimony to others already born. The group they immediately sought out included the apostles who (except for Thomas) had gathered together with other disciples. Undoubtedly, the women who had already played such a significant role in the day's stunning events were there. The two from Emmaus obviously knew that the disciples would be meeting together that evening and also knew the location of the meeting place. When they arrived they found the group discussing the Resurrection, saying that there was no doubt that Jesus had risen from the dead because he had also appeared unto Peter, their leader (Luke 24:34). Cleopas and his companion then added their witness and "told what things were done in the way, and how he [Jesus] was known of them in breaking of bread" (Luke 24:35).

SUNDAY EVENING'S PRIVATE MEETING

Back together again after an exhausting day (remember, all that we have described to this point happened on the same day), the disciples had sequestered themselves behind closed doors in a secret meeting Easter Sunday night. They feared what the Jewish leaders might do to followers of Jesus in view of the day's happenings (John 20:19). The meeting place is believed to be an upper room, "perhaps the same room, in the home of John Mark, where Jesus and the Twelve celebrated the Feast of the Passover" just three days before (McConkie, *Mortal Messiah*, 4:278).

As the disciples were sitting around during dinner and talk-ing about Jesus' resurrection (Mark 16:14), they may have even speculated about what all of this meant for the future of the Church, the direction of the kingdom of God which Jesus had often spoken of, and the restoration of Israel (Acts 1:6). While engaged in such sacred and significant conversations, "Jesus him-self stood in the midst of them, and saith unto them, Peace be unto you" (Luke 24:36). This greeting, *shalom aleikem,* was the traditional Hebrew exchange between close associates and was reported verbatim by both Luke and John (Luke 24:36; John 20:19). It remains an important expression of comradery and welcome among Jewish people today and was given new significance among Jesus' followers by the reality of the Resurrection.

We can well imagine the consternation this sudden appear-ance of Jesus caused among those in a room whose doors had remained shut the whole time. Luke indicates that even though the Savior offered the traditional and affectionate greeting, some of the disciples (he does not mention which ones) "were terrified and affrighted, and supposed that they had seen a spirit" (Luke 24:37). It is surprising that there was still such fear and lack of faith among some of the disciples, given all that had been reported that day regarding the Savior's resurrection, and all that had actually been seen by others of the company. But apparently there was, for Jesus "upbraided them with their unbelief and hardness of heart, because they believed not them which had seen him after he was risen" (Mark 16:14). Admittedly, even among those who believed in the Resurrection, such a visitation would have caused most, if not all, to be startled. But Luke and Mark are reporting something deeper—a fundamental lack of faith on the part of some disciples. Hence, the Savior's chastisement.

Ever the exemplar, Jesus rebuked their unbelief with sharpness (clarity), in harmony with the pattern he himself revealed in modern revelation (D&C 121:43). And then he proceeded to manifest his mercy, love, and patience to them so that their faith could increase and their knowledge of his resurrection become certain. He spoke to them as a parent might speak to calm the fear of a child and explain the situation that was causing the fear. It has been well said that usually we fear what we do not understand. I think this was true for the unbelieving disciples in the upper room that first Easter Sunday evening. I think we detect this in the Savior's patient and kind explanation as well as his demonstration to those assembled in the room. "And he said unto them, Why are ye troubled? and why do thoughts arise in your hearts? Behold my hands and my feet, that it is I myself: handle me, and see; for a spirit hath not flesh and bones, as ye see me have. And when he had thus spoken, he shewed them his hands and his feet" (Luke 24:38–40).

The Savior's invitation to handle his hands, feet, and side (John 20:20) was undoubtedly aimed at showing the disciples the very real wounds left in his body by the nails and the spear when he hung on the cross. Such tokens of his suffering would not be tangible if he were merely a spirit or a ghostly apparition.

John adds poignantly that after the Savior showed them his hands, his feet, and his side, "then were the disciples glad, when they saw the Lord" (John 20:20). One suspects that the word "glad" is a monumental understatement, but sometimes human language is simply inadequate to describe emotions and feelings of such overwhelming magnitude.

Luke's more detailed narrative of the Sunday evening meeting indicates that some of the disciples still had difficulty believing that Jesus had returned from the dead with his physical body reinvigorated. Luke's comment indicates that the doubters may not have wanted to let themselves believe in the miraculous event lest their joy be dashed once more if it proved to be false: "They yet believed not for joy, and wondered" (Luke 24:41). After all, they had put their trust in Jesus' messianic claims once before (though they misunderstood the nature of his messiahship) and undoubtedly felt betrayed when their Master was executed.

Jesus patiently continued to work with them in order to dispel their persistent disbelief. He asked for food and demonstrated that he was a genuine physical entity with a body capable of eating a piece of broiled fish and some honeycomb. This is extremely instructive to modern disciples, just as it was to the ancients, for we also now know that resurrected bodies think and speak and act and can perform physical functions, like eating (Luke 24:41–43). As Elder Talmage notes, "These unquestionable evidences of their Visitant's corporeity calmed and made rational the minds of the disciples" (*Jesus the Christ*, 688). They were now composed and receptive and could be taught with a quickened understanding as they stood or sat in their Master's presence. They could now comprehend his divinity as never before.

Having demonstrated physically that he was the resurrected Lord, Jesus next reinforced spiritually that he was the promised Messiah. He opened the scriptures to their understanding as he had done previously and refreshed their memories of past promises and teachings: "Thus it is written, and thus it behoved Christ to suffer, and to rise from the dead the third day" (Luke 24:46). He then reviewed the plan of salvation, emphasizing that his redeeming mission, his atonement, and his resurrection meant "that repentance and remission of sins should be preached in his name among all nations, beginning at Jerusalem" (Luke 24:47). Finally, the Savior reiterated to the disciples, especially the apostles, that they bore a special responsibility: "And ye are witnesses of these things" (Luke 24:48).

Though Jesus himself had said during his mortal ministry that he was not sent to any group except the house of Israel (Matthew 15:24), the risen Lord now foreshadowed a worldwide missionary effort. The twin messages of salvation and resurrection in Christ were to go to "all nations" not just to the Jewish people. They were to be carried forth by the witnesses who were in that upper room that Sunday night. They were to begin in Jerusalem and spread out to the world. The messages were to be sealed by the testimonies of the disciples. No plainer or more exciting directive was ever given by anyone. The missionary thrust of the Lord's Church was affirmed. That same directive has been reconfirmed in our day. For many Latter-day Saints, missionary labors are among the most rewarding experiences they have ever had.

Surely, there has never been a more patient, kind, consistent, or pedagogically sound teacher than Jesus. He was and is the perfect teacher and modeled the teaching techniques and attributes that all of us should strive to adopt; attributes that, if practiced, would bless our own family and friends immeasurably. In fact, I believe that if each of us were to try to practice the characteristics and techniques of the Master Teacher—cognitive, affective, and motor skill instruction—the progress of our students would be phenomenal. Jesus expanded the mind as well as the heart. He taught by precept as well as by example. He asked his students to think as well as to feel. He required the use of all the five human senses in the learning process.

Once *all* the disciples that Sunday night came to the realization that what they were seeing was real—that Jesus really had overcome death, that he truly was resurrected, that he was Israel's Messiah, who possessed genuine power over life and death—the Savior then repeated again the traditional greeting of welcome and blessing that he had uttered before, as if he were greeting them afresh, welcoming them into an entirely new way of thinking, a new circle of association, and a new realm of discipleship. *Shalom aleikhem*—"Peace be unto you: as my Father hath sent me, even so send I you" (John 20:21). This latter commission applied especially to the apostles in the room.

All of the disciples who had assembled that night in secret, behind closed doors, were now different, changed forevermore. They knew for certain of the fulfillment of promises made in Israel's distant past. They were all eyewitnesses of the resurrection of Jesus the Messiah. Eleven of them, however, would bear an extra burden as "special witnesses of the name of Christ in all the world" (D&C 107:23). A twelfth would soon be named to fill the vacancy left by Judas's betrayal and subsequent death.

The qualifications necessary for Judas's replacement were outlined a short time later by Luke when the eleven apostles met to fill the vacancy. Luke reported these qualifications and requirements in the sequel to his Gospel record, the Acts of the Apostles: "Wherefore of these men which have companied with us all the time that the Lord Jesus went in and out among us, Beginning from the baptism of John, unto that same day that he was taken up from us, must one be ordained to be a witness with us of his resurrection. And they appointed two, Joseph called Barsabas, who was surnamed Justus, and Matthias" (Acts 1:21–23). Luke is telling us that two men were found to possess the necessary basic qualifications and that one of whom would actually be called and ordained. The two men were chosen as candidates because they also had been with the Twelve from the beginning. Thus, I believe both Matthias and Barsabas Justus were in the upper room with the apostles and other disciples on the night of Jesus' resurrection.

A FITTING END TO RESURRECTION SUNDAY

The last thing Jesus did that Sunday night of which we have record was the bestowing of the gift of the Holy Ghost. Whether he performed the ordinance for all those assembled or just the apostles, we do not know explicitly, though I am inclined to believe it was only the apostles. John's record is ambiguous on this point and, in fact, the language he uses to describe the circumstances could be misunderstood if we did not know he was using a play on words. John records: "And when he had said this, he breathed on them, and saith unto them, Receive ye the Holy Ghost" (John 20:22). In Hebrew and in Aramaic, which

Jesus spoke, the word for "breath" is the same as the word for "spirit," as in the phrase "Holy Spirit." Thus, John was saying that Jesus used his holy breath (spirit) to give the Holy Spirit, or Holy Ghost.

It is clear from Luke's record of the postresurrection Church (the Acts of the Apostles) that the apostles began to possess the actual power of the Holy Ghost only on the day of Pentecost and afterward (Acts 2). What then did Jesus give to the apostles that Sunday evening? Elder Bruce R. McConkie helps us to understand that the realization of blessings or promises associated with an ordinance may not come until an appreciable amount of time has elapsed after the performance of the ordinance:

> From the time of John to this hour when the resurrected Lord stood before his apostolic witnesses, the only legally performed baptisms had been in water, with the promise in each instance of a future baptism of fire. Now the time was at hand to perform the ordinance which would entitle the saints to receive the baptism of fire. And so Jesus "breathed on them," which probably means that he laid his hands upon them as he uttered the decree: "Receive the Holy Ghost."
>
> They thus *received*, but did not at that moment actually *enjoy*, the gift of the Holy Ghost. . . . This gift offers certain blessings provided there is full compliance with the law involved; everyone upon whom the gift is bestowed does not in fact enjoy or possess the offered gift. In the case of the apostles the actual enjoyment of the gift was delayed until the day of Pentecost (Acts 2). . . .

The saints in this day go through the ordinance of the laying on of hands which gives them the gift, which by definition is the right to receive the companionship of the Spirit. *If and when they are worthy*, they are then immersed in the Spirit, as it were, thus actually enjoying the gift. (*Doctrinal New Testament Commentary*, 1:856–57; emphasis added)

The enjoyment of promises and blessings associated with any ordinance are always predicated on worthiness as well as the Lord's timetable. Individuals may participate in an ordinance but not have the terms and conditions of the ordinance become effective until they are worthy.

The ratification of any ordinance, and thus the realization of its associated promises and blessings, comes through the Holy Spirit of Promise (D&C 132:7). He knows when we are worthy and capable of enjoying those blessings and promises. This is for our protection and benefit. It is a great burden to be held accountable for knowledge and power and blessings that we are not ready or able to handle appropriately. The Holy Ghost also knows the Lord's timetable. He helps to implement it. And so even though the disciples participated in the ordinance of the gift of the Holy Ghost that Easter Sunday night, they did not enjoy the full blessings until the day of Pentecost, fifty days after Passover.

To his servants gathered in the upper room the Sunday night of his resurrection, Jesus also promised the power to remit people's sins or to retain them: "Whose soever sins ye remit, they are remitted unto them; and whose soever sins ye retain, they are retained" (John 20:23).

In a sense, that is implicit in the gospel plan. Remission of sins comes through the principles and ordinances that the apostles, seventies, and elders teach and implement throughout the world. "Thus the legal administrators who preach the gospel have power to remit the sins of men in the waters of baptism, and they have power to retain the sins of those who do not repent and are not baptized for the remission of sins" (McConkie, *Mortal Messiah*, 4:283). There is another sense in which the early Church leaders would possess the power to remit or retain sins. The Twelve, as prophets, seers, and revelators, had the power to direct the Lord's Church. They held the keys of the kingdom of heaven to bind on earth and in heaven and to seal or unseal on earth and in heaven (Matthew 16:19). This is true for our present dispensation as well.

LEAVING THE DISCIPLES

Having confirmed the reality of his literal resurrection and born witness that he was the fulfilment of the promises in the scriptures, Jesus left the disciples for a time, undoubtedly to ponder what they each had experienced. So very much had happened during that first Easter Sunday, not the least of which was the turning of doubt and fear into certainty and joy. Even those among the disciples who had resisted believing in the literal resurrection were healed of their spiritual malady by the power of pure knowledge and revelation.

Modern disciples must resist the temptation to judge these ancient followers of Christ too harshly. They had to deal with events and circumstances that were completely beyond their (or anyone else's) realm of experience. Jesus' crucifixion was so horrible and these disciples had been hurt so badly (spiritually, emotionally, and psychologically) over Jesus' execution after they had sacrificed so much for his cause that we ought to marvel at the strength and courage they demonstrated. Many of us can scarcely fathom the challenges they faced. Jerusalem was a volatile place, and they were putting themselves at risk by simply continuing to meet together as followers of Jesus. But they came through it all right and in just a few weeks' time became the greatest force for good, as well as for change, the world has ever known.

The former treatise have I made, O Theophilus, of all that Jesus began both to do and teach,

Until the day in which he was taken up, after that he through the Holy Ghost had given commandments unto the apostles whom he had chosen:

To whom also he shewed himself alive after his passion by many infallible proofs, being seen of them forty days, and speaking of the things pertaining to the kingdom of God.

ACTS 1:1–3

CHAPTER 7

Beginning His Forty-Day Ministry

itnesses of the resurrection of Jesus Christ grew in number and certitude immediately following Resurrection Sunday as Jesus returned on several occasions to instruct his special witnesses and friends whom he had commissioned to lead the Church after his ascension. It is the period known in ecclesiastical history as the forty-day ministry. As Luke testified, Jesus "shewed himself alive [to the apostles] after his passion by many infallible proofs, being seen of them *forty days,* and speaking of the things pertaining to the kingdom of God (Acts 1:3; emphasis added).

"DOUBTING" THOMAS

Among the first to whom Jesus appeared after his initial visits of Resurrection Sunday was the apostle Thomas. This important leader was completely absent during all of Jesus' appearances to his disciples on that most important Sunday. Scripture does not tell us why or where he was, only that he "was not with them when Jesus came" (John 20:24).

Thomas was one of the original Twelve. His name in Hebrew

and Aramaic means "twin" and thus is translated by the Greek *Didymus* ("twin") in John 11:16. Little is recorded of Thomas in the Gospels, though John's record tells us more about his personality than that of some of the other apostles. One tradition holds that he was the twin brother of Matthew. Another says Thomas was the twin of James. We do not know for sure. Thomas's name appears in all the lists of the Twelve in the synoptic Gospels (Matthew 10:3; Mark 3:18; Luke 6:15; compare Acts 1:13). The episode for which he is best known and the one which has encumbered him with his lasting moniker, "Doubting Thomas," stems from his absence from the Quorum of the Twelve Apostles on Resurrection Sunday and his subsequent attitude toward reports of Jesus' resurrection.

Only John recounts the story of Thomas's revelatory experience. When he got back with his brethren, the other apostles informed Thomas that they had seen the Lord—alive! "But he said unto them, Except I shall see in his hands the print of the nails, and put my finger into the print of the nails, and thrust my hand into his side, I will not believe" (John 20:25).

It is truly unfortunate that the only thing most people associate with Thomas is doubt. Though he was skeptical, it should also be remembered that he was extremely brave and possessed a noble character, if somewhat tinged with pessimism. Earlier, during Jesus' mortal ministry, when the Savior announced his intention of going to Bethany of Judea to visit the home of Lazarus, Thomas brushed aside the protests of the other disciples who warned that Jesus' life was in danger there (though they may have been more worried about their own vulnerability than anything else). Thomas answered his associates, "Let us also go, that we may die with him" (John 11:16). Even if Thomas was looking for the worst in this situation, he had good reason.

Jewish leaders in Jerusalem really were plotting to kill Jesus, and Bethany was right next door to the capital city.

It is no wonder that Thomas was pessimistic. He seems to have realized early that Jesus was headed for disaster in Judea when not everyone understood the full gravity of the circumstances. The others might have believed that Jewish leaders would *try* to harm their Master, but it seems unlikely to me that very many actually believed their Messiah could be mortally wounded. In fact, President Wilford Woodruff confirmed this lack of understanding on the part of most of the ancient apostles when he said: "I remember very well the last charge that Joseph [Smith] gave to the Apostles. We had as little idea that he was going from us as the Apostles of the Savior did that He was going to be taken from them. Joseph talked with us as plainly as did the Savior to His Apostles, but we did not understand that he was about to depart from us any more than the Apostles understood the Savior" (*Collected Discourses,* 188).

Thomas's realism, and also his strength of character, showed through during the incident with Lazarus when he stood by the wishes of his Master and told the others they should too, even if it meant dying with Jesus. Of course, it is also fair to say that Thomas himself did not fully understand all that Jesus was really saying when he spoke of his redemptive mission. John records an episode where Jesus used Thomas's lack of understanding to teach a valuable lesson:

> And if I go and prepare a place for you, I will come again, and receive you unto myself; that where I am, there you may be also.
>
> And wither I go ye know, and the way ye know.

Thomas saith unto him, Lord, we know not wither thou goest; and how can we know the way?

Jesus saith unto him, I am the way, the truth, and the life; no man cometh unto the Father, but by me.

If ye had known me, ye should have known my Father also: and from henceforth ye know him, and have seen him. (John 14:3–7)

Therefore, it seems understandable to me that when Jesus' resurrection did occur, Thomas had trouble accepting the word of his colleagues. He himself did not comprehend the true nature and power of Jesus' messiahship. He was also a realist, perhaps a pessimist, but that is what recent experience had taught him. The Savior's crucifixion had confirmed his suspicions and, perhaps more significantly, hurt him deeply. Thomas's bluntly stated personal requirement of needing to feel the nail wounds and the spear wound shows just how well he knew what had happened on the cross and just how painfully and exquisitely the image of his dead Master had been imprinted on his soul. It was not that he mistrusted the testimony of his associates, exactly, but rather that he was dubious about their interpretation of "resurrection" their insistence on "the literal and corporeal nature of it" (McConkie, *Doctrinal New Testament Commentary*, 1:860). After all, he knew without a doubt that Jesus had died a horrible death, and he could see no tangible sign of the establishment of a great and powerful (politically and militarily speaking) messianic kingdom that was to accompany an era of resurrection.

Exactly a week after the Resurrection, the apostles were met together again with Thomas in attendance. It was Sunday, the new Sabbath commemorating the Resurrection, and the doors were again shut. Just as he had done before, Jesus came through solid element, stood in the midst of them, and reiterated the greeting of warmth and affection: *Shalom aleikhem*—"Peace be unto you" (John 20:26).

It is obvious that the Savior knew of the earlier exchange between Thomas and his colleagues in the Quorum of the Twelve Apostles. For after greeting all of them, he immediately singled out Thomas and presented the proof that left no doubt. "Then saith he to Thomas, Reach hither thy finger, and behold my hands; and reach hither thy hand, and thrust it into my side: and be not faithless, but believing" (John 20:27).

Many, if not most, students of the New Testament have pondered the power and profundity of this moment in time. It is, in my view, captured perfectly by John's brief but poignant report: "Thomas answered and said unto him, My Lord and my God" (John 20:28). Thomas now knew for himself that Jesus was the promised Messiah; that Jesus was literally, physically alive again with a body of flesh and bone. All doubt, fear, hurt, and pessimism were swept away. Nonbiblical texts affirm that once Thomas was given the sure witness he said he required, his loyalty and dedication were beyond question. He became a stalwart in the kingdom.

Some may wonder how it is that on the one hand the Lord and his prophets have so often roundly denounced sign-seeking individuals and generations (Matthew 12:39; Jacob 7:13–20; Alma 30:48–60) but on the other have sanctioned the giving of a sign to Thomas when he clearly sought it. Perhaps some resolution of this seeming contradiction is to be found in the word of the Lord as given through the Prophet Joseph Smith. He declared that signs will follow faith: those who possess basic faith, or even a desire to believe, will be rewarded (D&C 63:7–11; Moroni 10:4–5; Alma 32:27). Thomas's faith may have been weakened after Jesus' crucifixion, but he did not lose it. One suspects that he strongly desired to believe in the Resurrection all along, even if he was overcome by skepticism for a time. In the end, he was rewarded for his previous, as well as his continuing, commitment to the Church in the face of great difficulty and grave danger. This, after all, is the essence of faith—doing what we *believe* is right in the face of challenges, walking to the edge of the light and then taking one more step, trusting God that the light will move with us.

How like Thomas are many of us at one time or another in our lives. Overcoming doubt is part of the test of our mortal probation. In fact, I dare say that very few come to the position of authentic assurance without first serving an apprenticeship in uncertainty. God wants to be our mentor and tutor, and he loves to see our change and rebirth. He delights in rewarding our faith. He "delight[s] to honor those who serve [him] in righteousness. . . . Great shall be their reward and eternal shall be their glory" (D&C 76:5–6).

The promised reward for faith is, in fact, the principle underlying Jesus' parting instruction to Thomas and the other apostles that Sunday Sabbath one week after his resurrection. Our faith will be greatly rewarded. In truth, righteous action based on faith is of greater value in the Lord's eyes than righteous action based on knowledge. "Jesus saith unto him, Thomas, because thou hast seen me, thou hast believed: blessed are they that have not seen, and yet have believed" (John 20:29).

THE LAW OF RESTORATION

A singular and significant aspect of the doctrine of resurrection concerns the nature of the bodies with which we will all arise. Though Jesus came forth from the grave still possessing the wounds of his crucifixion and showed them to Thomas and the others, he is unique in this regard. All others will come forth having had their wounds, scars, imperfections, and deformities taken away. About one hundred years *before* Jesus arose from the dead, the prophet Alma testified that there would be no physical deformities in the resurrection: "The soul shall be restored to the body, and the body to the soul; yea, and every limb and joint shall be restored to its body; yea, even a hair of the head shall not be lost; but all things shall be restored to their proper and perfect frame" (Alma 40:23).

The perfect nature of our physical bodies in the resurrection is part of the sweeping law of restoration. Yet, the nature of our spirits, the very core of our beings, will not instantly and automatically conform to the nature of our bodies, will not become pure and perfect just because we have passed beyond this mortal sphere. If we have not repented and desired to change while in this life, the "same spirit which doth possess [our] bodies at the time that [we] go out of this life, that same spirit will have power to possess [our] body in that eternal world" (Alma 34:34). This too is part of the grand law of restoration. "When a person rises in the resurrection, his body will be perfect but that does not mean that he will be perfect in faith. There will be different kinds of bodies in the resurrection—celestial, terrestrial, and telestial—and they will not be alike. . . . Every man will receive according to his works" (Smith, *Doctrines of Salvation*, 2:292).

The Book of Mormon is our greatest testament of the doctrine of the resurrection and the restoration that it brings about. The prophets of the Book of Mormon generally speak of three types of restoration that the resurrection is responsible for: the restoration of the spirit to the physical body; the restoration of all people to the presence of God to be judged; and the restoration of our individual memories. Nothing can compare to the power of the resurrection and the changes enacted by it, and nobody summarizes this truth better than Amulek:

> Behold, the day cometh that all shall rise from the dead and stand before God, and be judged according to their works.
>
> Now, there is a death which is called a temporal death; and the death of Christ shall loose the bands of this temporal death, that all shall be raised from this temporal death.
>
> The spirit and the body shall be reunited again in its perfect form; both limb and joint shall be restored to its proper frame, even as we now are at this time; and we shall be brought to stand before God, knowing even as we know now, and have a bright recollection of all our guilt.
>
> Now, this restoration shall come to all, both old and young, both bond and free, both male and female, both the wicked and the righteous; and even there shall not so much as a hair of their heads be lost; but every thing shall be restored to its perfect frame, as it is now, or in the body, and shall be brought and be arraigned before the bar of Christ the Son, and God the Father, and the Holy Spirit, which is one Eternal God, to be judged according to their works, whether they be good or whether they be evil.
>
> Now, behold, I have spoken unto you concerning the death of the mortal body, and also concerning the resurrection of the mortal body. I say unto you that this mortal body is raised to an immortal body, that is from death,

even from the first death unto life, that they can die no more; their spirits uniting with their bodies, never to be divided; thus the whole becoming spiritual and immortal, that they can no more see corruption. (Alma 11:41–45)

Similarly, President Joseph Fielding Smith, a modern prophet, left no doubt that one of the greatest blessings accruing to us as a free gift resulting from the Savior's redemption is a restored body—a body without deformities—in the resurrection: "When we come forth from the dead, our spirits and bodies will be reunited inseparably, never again to be divided, and they will then be assigned to the kingdom to which they belong. All deformities and imperfections will be removed, and the body will conform to the likeness of the spirit" (*Doctrines of Salvation*, 2:289).

Nowhere is the Savior's mercy and grace shown more forcefully than in the doctrine of resurrection. Through the infinite power of Christ's atonement and resurrection, every man, woman, and child will come forth from the grave at the time of their appointed resurrection and be instantly healed of any physical defects they may have struggled with in mortality. President Joseph Fielding Smith also stated:

Bodies will come up, of course, as they were laid down, but will be restored to their proper, perfect frame immediately. Old people will not look old when they come forth from the grave. Scars will be removed. No one will be bent or wrinkled. . . . Each body will come forth with its perfect frame. If there has been some deformity or physical impairment in this life, it will be removed.

The Lord is not impotent to heal and restore the dead to their perfect frame in the resurrection. If the Savior could restore withered hands, eyes that had never had sight, crooked bodies, in this mortal life, surely the Father will not permit bodies that are not physically perfect to come forth in the resurrection. (*Doctrines of Salvation*, 2:292–93)

Over the years I have had the privilege of teaching a student or two who shared with me their witness of the truth of President Smith's teachings. They have seen, in a dream or vision or by personal revelation, a relative who had lost an arm or leg in mortality or who faced some other physical challenge, stand healed and whole in the resurrection—without any physical deformities. These have been profound tutorials for me, the supposed professor. I quote from an essay written by one of these students:

In or about 1967 my uncle lost his right arm (at the shoulder) in a farming accident. I have no memory of him with his arm. My earliest memory of him was the first time I saw him after the accident.

Years later (1979), one of my aunts died. During her funeral I was sitting in front of my mother, who was seated on my uncle's right side. At some point in the meeting I turned to check on my mother. I could not believe what I saw. At first I wondered what was wrong with what I saw. When I figured it out, I turned again to double-check what I was experiencing. I saw my uncle's right arm around my mother, with his hand wrapped around her right shoulder. This "vision" continued through the entire funeral service. When I told my mother about this experience, she replied that if he had had his arm, that is exactly where it would have been. . . .

Because of this experience I *know* that the body parts will be restored and that deformities will be fixed. I know that our spirits are in perfect form and that is what our bodies will be perfected to when that transition is made.

THE SAVIOR'S WOUNDS

What is true for all humankind concerning wounds was not true for the Savior, and thus in this respect "we must not judge the resurrection of others by the resurrection of Jesus Christ" (Smith, *Doctrines of Salvation*, 2:290). Jesus retained the wounds of his crucifixion so he could identify himself to others in the meridian dispensation with absolute clarity. Thus, Thomas saw and felt those wounds.

Likewise, at his second coming, when Jesus comes to his own people, the Jews, who are still on the earth at a time of unparalleled distress, he will show to all assembled the wounds in his hands and feet, and they will know that he has always been their Messiah as well as their King. He declared: "And then shall the Jews look upon me and say: What are these wounds in thine hands and in thy feet? Then shall they know that I am the Lord; for I will say unto them: These wounds are the wounds with which I was wounded in the house of my friends. I am he who was lifted up. I am Jesus that was crucified. I am the Son of God. And then shall they weep because of their iniquities; then shall they lament because they persecuted their king" (D&C 45:51–53). This same prophecy was also given to the Old Testament prophet Zechariah (Zechariah 12:9–14; 13:1–9; 14:1–21).

Here again we see that Jesus "doeth not anything save it be for the benefit of the world" (2 Nephi 26:24). Elder Jeffrey R. Holland poignantly reminds us that "Jesus has chosen, even in a resurrected, otherwise perfected body, to retain *for the benefit of His disciples* the wounds in His hands and in His feet and in His side. . . . These wounds are the principal way we are to recognize Him when He comes" (*"Therefore, What?"* 9; emphasis added). Elder Holland reminds us that these wounds are reminders that painful things happen to even the pure and the perfect in mortality. Paradoxically, he who yet bears the scars and lesions of obedience and sacrifice will heal us of our pains and wounds!

CHILDREN AND THE RESURRECTION

In his writings and teachings, President Joseph Fielding Smith clarified a misunderstanding about the Resurrection that derived from a sermon given by his father, President Joseph F. Smith, sixth president of The Church of Jesus Christ of Latter-day Saints. The latter, when speaking at the funeral sermon of Sister Rachel Grant, said that she would be resurrected in the same form and likeness as she was laid to rest, "even to the wounds in the flesh. Not that a person will always be marred by scars, wounds, deformities, defects or infirmities, for these will be removed in their course, in their proper time, according to the merciful providence of God" (*Gospel Doctrine*, 23).

President Joseph Fielding Smith said of his father's statement:

> While he expresses the thought that *the body will come forth as it was laid down,* he also expresses the thought that it will take time to adjust the body from the condition of imperfections. This, of course, is reasonable,

but at the same time the length of time to make these adjustments will not cover an appreciable extent of time.

President Smith never intended to convey the thought that it would require weeks or months of time in order for the defects to be removed. These changes will come naturally, of course, but almost instantly. We cannot look upon it in any other way. For instance, a man who has lost a leg in childhood will have his leg restored. *It does not grow in the grave,* but will be restored naturally, but with the power of the Almighty it will not take extended time for this to be accomplished. (*Doctrines of Salvation,* 2:293–94; emphasis added)

While it is clear that there is no physical growth while our bodies are in the grave, by the same token there is a profound implication of this principle that has to do with children who pass on. Truly, it is one of the most sublime and comforting doctrines ever revealed. Children who have died will be resurrected and come forth as children, without defect or deformity, and their parents will have the privilege of raising them to adulthood. President Joseph F. Smith is one of our most reliable sources on this point. He said:

Joseph Smith taught the doctrine that the infant child that was laid away in death would come up in the resurrection as a child; and, pointing to the mother of a lifeless child, he said to her: "You will have the joy, the pleasure, and satisfaction of nurturing this child, after its resurrection, until it reaches the full stature of its spirit." There is restitution, there is growth, there is development, after the resurrection from death. I love this truth. It speaks volumes of happiness, of joy and gratitude to my soul. Thank the Lord he has revealed these principles to us. . . .

One day I was conversing with a brother-in-law of mine, Lorin Walker, who married my oldest sister. In the course of the conversation he happened to mention that he was present at the funeral of my cousin Sophronia, and that he heard the Prophet Joseph Smith declare the very words that Aunt Agnes had told me.

I said to him, "Lorin, what did the Prophet say?" and he repeated, as nearly as he could remember, what the Prophet Joseph said in relation to little children. The body remains undeveloped in the grave, but the spirit returns to God who gave it. Afterwards, in the resurrection, the spirit and body will be reunited; the body will develop and grow to the full stature of the spirit; and the resurrected soul will go on to perfection. So I had the statement of two witnesses who heard this doctrine announced by the Prophet Joseph Smith, the source of intelligence. (*Gospel Doctrine*, 455–56)

If such a doctrine could be heralded from the rooftops, it would bring amazing relief and soul-satisfying comfort to the many parents who have lost little ones. It is one of the most significant manifestations of God's love, Christ's infinite redeeming power, and the fairness of the law of justice, which guarantees recompense for the unfair circumstances of mortality. In the case of my own family, it serves as a motivation to all of us to live worthy of the company of a little girl, a sister who lived only three days before succumbing to the effects of a congenital heart defect. I am sure it was a source of great sadness to my parents. But by the power of the atonement and resurrection of Jesus

Christ, this little daughter and sister has already received a guarantee of exaltation. She has, in effect, inherited exaltation, though the full realization of all that means lies in the future. She will be resurrected as an infant for my parents to rear to adulthood. No price can be put on that kind of knowledge, which brings such comfort. No price will be able to be put on the feelings of gratitude and fulfillment that will be ours as we enjoy the company of our loved ones in the resurrection.

Years ago, as a full-time missionary, I had the privilege of teaching the doctrines of the Atonement and the exaltation of little children to a young couple who had unexpectedly lost an infant to an unknown cause of death. To this day, I vividly remember watching their great sorrow turn to exquisite joy as they came to know the truth—that their little one did not need baptism before death, did not need last rites, was not lost, but was an exalted being who was waiting for them on the other side of the veil. That was a profound experience for me. I still look back on it with some wonder.

I treasure the words of Elder Bruce R. McConkie, who summarizes the doctrine of salvation for little children and conveys my own deep feelings on this point:

> Among all the glorious gospel verities given of God to his people there is scarcely a doctrine so sweet, so soul satisfying, and so soul sanctifying, as the one which proclaims—Little children shall be saved. They are alive in Christ and shall have eternal life. For them the family unit will continue, and the fulness of exaltation is theirs. No blessing shall be withheld. They shall rise in immortal glory, grow to full maturity, and live forever in the highest heaven of the celestial kingdom—all through the merits

and mercy and grace of the Holy Messiah, all because of the atoning sacrifice of Him who died that we might live. ("Salvation of Little Children," 3)

Little children who die before the age of accountability receive exaltation. They will not be tested in paradise, during the Millennium, or after the Millennium has concluded. They are not subject to any "if" clauses (that is, they will receive exaltation if . . .) or further probation. Said Elder Bruce R. McConkie:

> Would the Lord test someone who cannot fail the test and whose exaltation is guaranteed? For that matter, all those billions of people who will be born during the millennium, when Satan is bound, "shall grow up without sin unto salvation" (D&C 45:58) and therefore will not be tested.
>
> Satan cannot tempt little children in this life, nor in the spirit world, nor after their resurrection. Little children who die before reaching the years of accountability will not be tempted (*Doctrines of Salvation*, 2:56–57). Such is the emphatic language of President Joseph Fielding Smith. ("Salvation of Little Children," 6)

In a general conference talk some years ago, President Thomas S. Monson recounted the touching story of Thomas and Sarah Hilton, who went to Samoa in 1892 to preside over the mission there. They took with them a baby daughter and were blessed by the birth of two sons while they served. Then tragedy struck. Within three years' time, all their children died, and in 1895 the Hiltons returned from their mission childless. One can hardly imagine a more sorrowful circumstance. Yet, there was faith in the midst of profound trials.

Elder David O. McKay of the Quorum of the Twelve was a friend of the family and deeply touched by their tragic loss. In 1921, as part of a world tour of the Church, he stopped in Samoa and, owing to a prior promise to the now-widowed Sister Hilton, personally visited the graves of the Hilton children. He wrote home to Sister Hilton:

Dear Sister Hilton:

Just as the descending rays of the late afternoon sun touched the tops of the tall coconut trees, Wednesday, May 18th, 1921, a party of five stood with bowed heads in front of the little Fagali'i Cemetery. . . . We were there, as you will remember, in response to a promise I made you before I left home.

The graves and headstones are in a good state of preservation. . . . I reproduce here a copy I made as I stood . . . outside the stone wall surrounding the spot.

Janette Hilton
Bn: Sept. 10, 1891
Died: June 4, 1892
"Rest, darling Jennie"

George Emmett Hilton
Bn: Oct. 12, 1894
Died: Oct. 19, 1894
"Peaceful be thy slumber"

Thomas Harold Hilton
Bn: Sept. 21, 1892
Died: March 17, 1894
"Rest on the hillside, rest"

As I looked at those three little graves, I tried to imagine the scenes through which you passed during your young motherhood here in old Samoa. As I did so, the little headstones became monuments not only to the little babies sleeping beneath them, but also to a mother's faith and devotion to the eternal principles of truth and life. Your three little ones, Sister Hilton, in silence most eloquent and effective, have continued to carry on your noble missionary work begun nearly 30 years ago, and they will continue as long as there are gentle hands to care for their last earthly resting place.

By loving hands their dying eyes were closed;
By loving hands their little limbs composed;
By foreign hands their humble graves adorned;
By strangers honored, and by strangers mourned.

Tofa Soifua,

David O. McKay

President Thomas S. Monson commented: "This touching account conveys to the grieving heart 'the peace . . . which passeth all understanding'" (*Ensign*, May 1998, 54).

Indeed, tragedy sometimes strikes in the midst of faithful service and sacrifice. But we may rest assured that no pain we are called to pass through will be endured alone. Often family or friends are there to support us, and in truth, the Savior will never forget us. More important, little children who die are not lost. The Savior's atonement guarantees that they will be exalted and so will their parents who endure their temporary loss in patience and faith.

The same principles of resurrection and exaltation that apply to little children who die before the age of accountability also apply to those who are mentally handicapped or developmentally challenged in mortality. They are raised to the status and stature of gods in the eternities. Said Elder Bruce R. McConkie:

> They never arrive at the years of accountability and are considered as though they were little children. If because of some physical deficiency, or for some other reason unknown to us, they never mature in the spiritual and moral sense, then they never become accountable for sins. They need no baptism; they are alive in Christ; and they will receive, inherit, and possess in eternity on the same basis as do all children.
>
> After revealing that little children are redeemed from the foundation of the world through the atoning sacrifice of Him who died to save us all, and after specifying that Satan has no power to tempt little children until they begin to become accountable, the Lord applied the same principles to those who are mentally deficient: "And, again, I say unto you, that whoso having knowledge, have I not commanded to repent? And he that hath no understanding, it remaineth in me to do according as it is written" (D&C 29:49–50). ("Salvation of Little Children," 6–7)

Nowhere is the meaning and message of Easter so clearly evident. Nowhere does it ring so triumphant as when we contemplate the Savior's power to bring about the resurrection and exaltation of little children. I am personally moved to tears when I realize that this aspect of the resurrection is only one dimension of the greatness of Jesus of Nazareth, the Messiah. What a different perspective we are given when we begin to understand more fully the Father's eternal plan, his mercy and goodness, and the incomparable power of the Son's atonement. Indeed, I am persuaded that we may have gotten some things backwards. Instead of feeling sorry for those who struggle with developmental disabilities, maybe we ought to feel bad that we weren't more valiant in our premortal life and thereby worthy of the same immediate guarantee of exaltation that is given to little children and individuals with developmental challenges.

AT THE SEA OF TIBERIAS

After a time, the apostolic witnesses of Jesus' resurrection left Jerusalem and went back to their homeland, the Galilee region in the north. They returned there because, by prior arrangement, they had an appointment to keep with Jesus, who said he would appear to them in Galilee (Matthew 28:10). Perhaps in waiting for this visit, or feeling frustrated over not knowing exactly what to do next, Peter announced to his associates that he was going fishing (John 21:3).

It is not hard to understand Peter's actions. He probably felt adrift. For three years he had followed Jesus, relied on him for instruction, and depended on him for spiritual nourishment and direction. Now Jesus was gone and with him, so was Peter's personal anchor. He understandably felt he needed further instruction and wasn't getting it. He therefore returned to the one thing he knew to do, the one thing that would at least provide for the temporal and physical needs of the group, the one sure thing in his life after so much of his world had been turned upside down.

With Peter at that time were six of the eleven apostles: James and John (the sons of Zebedee), Thomas and Nathanael, and two unnamed individuals—perhaps Andrew and Philip "since those two had been engaged with Peter and the others in like ventures in earlier days" (McConkie, *Mortal Messiah*, 4:288). These all said to Peter, "We also go with thee," and immediately they entered the ship (John 21:3).

Luke and Mark confirm the basic accuracy of John's account. Fishing on the Sea of Galilee was a well-organized enterprise among the families represented by the apostles who were with Peter. Peter and Andrew, brothers, worked in a partnership with James and John, the sons of Zebedee, and they supervised hired hands (Luke 5:7–10; Mark 1:20). They owned their own boats (Luke 5:11), and thus it wasn't hard for them to find a vessel to go fishing in. Fishing could be a fairly rewarding business. Meat was expensive in antiquity, and fish was an important commodity and major source of protein for most families living around the Sea of Galilee (also called the Sea of Tiberias). The term *Galilee* derives from a Hebrew word meaning "ring." There were many more villages ringing the lake in ancient times than today. For Peter and the others, the lure of their previous vocation would not have been inconsequential after Jesus was gone.

John tells us that the apostles toiled all night on the Sea of Galilee but caught nothing. As dawn broke, they saw a man standing on the shore, though they did not know it was their Master. He asked them about their success and told them to cast their nets on the starboard side of the boat. Their catch turned out to be phenomenal, so great that they could not pull in the net, all because they were willing to listen to One wiser than they. John was the first to recognize Jesus and announced to Peter, "It is the Lord" (John 21:7). So excited was Peter to see his Master that he jumped into the water and made his way to shore. The others also came in the "little ship," dragging the fish-laden net in the water behind the boat (John 21:8).

Living in the Holy Land myself, I came to appreciate John's

account so much more. It has come alive for me because of images still to be seen on the Sea of Galilee, images that provide windows to the past. Fishing companies headquartered on the shores of Galilee still send their boats out at night, and they fish till dawn. Some fishermen still partially strip, as Peter did, when they're working their catch. And a first-century boat can now be seen in a museum built close to the western shore of the sea.

In one of the more spectacular finds of the late twentieth century, archaeologists in 1986 recovered from the muddy bottom of the northwestern sector of the Sea of Galilee a boat from the first century after Christ. Indeed, it seems "little," to use John's term, for a commercial fishing vessel; however, it was well-made and gives us a good idea of what the fishing and ship-building industries were like in the days of Jesus. Shipwrights in antiquity went about building their ships differently from the way wooden ships were built in more recent times. In modern construction the keel was laid down, the ribs attached, and then the hull planking nailed to the ribs ("skeleton-first" construction). In Jesus' time, however, the keel was laid down first and then the hull built around it with the ribs affixed afterward ("shell-first" construction). Such was the construction of the boat found in 1986 dating from the general time period of the Savior and the apostles. The excavation and preservation of this boat, which had been under water for approximately two millennia, constitute a remarkable story. It is wonderfully illuminating to see this boat. It helps us to better visualize the events and feel closer to the people described in John's Gospel (Wachsman, *Sea of Galilee Boat*). It reminds us that the scene described by John really did happen.

LESSONS IN SERVANT LEADERSHIP

As soon as all the apostles had reached the shore, they found that a bed of hot coals had been prepared and fish were cooking thereon, with fresh bread ready. Jesus then treated his friends to a hot meal (John 21:9, 12–13). Though the Savior would yet use the occasion to teach powerful lessons, the story up to this point is full of profound meaning. From his suggestion to these brethren to cast their nets in a certain location, we see that Jesus did indeed care about their temporal well-being, just as he cares about the temporal well-being of his disciples and Saints today (John 21:5–6). And like the ancient apostles, we have to be willing to listen to him.

Just as it was heartwarming for the apostles then to realize that their Master had not stopped caring about their temporal needs, it is heartwarming now to realize that he cares about our having sufficient for our needs. Just as he knew where the fish were located in the sea, so he knows how we can be happy and what we must do to take advantage of his wisdom. It is important to note that Jesus did *not* do the fishing for his apostles. But he helped them focus their energy so they could be successful.

Ever the servant, Jesus prepared a warm place of rest for his apostles and then cooked a meal for them (John 21:9, 12–13). He cooked for them! What a stunning image this presented—the King of the Jews, the Savior of the World, the Master of the Universe, the very Son of God, the Great Jehovah—prepared a fire and cooked some food for his disciples because they were cold and tired and hungry. We must be clear about this. Jesus was God! He was the Redeemer of all. He had already performed the most significant and profound act of service in the history of Creation: the Atonement. He had already opened the door to an eternity's worth of possibilities for the whole human family, and yet he wanted to make dinner, to make his disciples happy, because they were cold and tired and hungry! It was not beneath his dignity to care for their personal needs, to warm them and make them feel comfortable and valued. He truly modeled what he taught; he who was the greatest made himself to be the least and the servant of all (Matthew 23:11).

Having shown by his actions the way of perfect servant-leadership, Jesus was ready to teach with words. In this atmosphere of total service, and against the backdrop of his personal example of selfless concern for others, Jesus instructed the chief apostle, Peter, as to what he must do for the rest of his life. Using the draft of fish as the object lesson, fish he had helped Peter catch, Jesus taught Peter that he was to leave fishing, leave economic pursuits, and feed the Savior's sheep just as the Savior had fed him that morning (John 21:9–17). Jesus would take care of Peter as he had that morning, but Peter was to take care of the Church. The rest of the New Testament record shows us that this lesson was not lost on the chief apostle.

As if to confirm in Peter's mind that his was now a call to imitate the totally selfless life of his Master, Jesus next foretold of Peter's own death. "Verily, verily, I say unto thee, When thou wast young, thou girdedst thyself, and walkedst whither thou wouldest: but when thou shalt be old, thou shalt stretch forth thy hands, and another shall gird thee, and carry thee whither thou wouldest not" (John 21:18). Of this verse Elder Talmage notes, "John informs us that the Lord so spake signifying the death by which Peter should find a place among the martyrs; the analogy points to crucifixion, and traditional history is without contradiction as to this being the death by which Peter sealed his testimony of the Christ" (*Jesus the Christ*, 693).

Finally, Jesus put the capstone on the morning's instruction. He simply but bluntly commanded Peter, "Follow me" (John 21:19). According to reputable tradition, recorded in the statements of various early authorities of the Christian Church, Peter did follow Jesus. His death fulfilled the prophecy of the Savior. The chief apostle died in Rome—martyred in the last years of the reign of Emperor Nero (A.D. 67–68). In a nonbiblical text, 1 Clement 5:4, it is said of Peter that he suffered not one or two but many trials, and having given his testimony, he went to the place which was his due. Ignatius, bishop of Antioch, refers to the deaths of Peter and Paul in Rome, as does Eusebius of Caesarea. Tertullian refers to three martyrdoms at Rome: Peter, Paul, and John. And, finally, Origen reported that Peter "at the end . . . came to Rome and was crucified head downwards" (Eusebius, *Ecclesiastical History*, 3.1.2). To the very end, Peter followed his Lord and Master in both word and deed. He acted like him, taught like him, was rejected like him, and in the end suffered the same kind of ignominious death.

The last exchange between Jesus and Peter during this, the third visitation of the Savior to an assembled group of disciples in the Holy Land (John 21:14), concerned the destiny of the apostle John. As Jesus and Peter walked together, and Peter contemplated his Master's prophecy that he, the chief apostle, would follow Jesus to a cross, he looked back and saw John following. "Peter seeing him saith to Jesus, Lord, and what shall this man do?" (John 21:21). That Peter's question may have derived from motives not entirely pure seems evident in Jesus' mild rebuke. "If I will that he tarry till I come, what is that to thee? Follow thou me" (John 21:22).

This exhortation that Peter should follow the course outlined for him and stop worrying about what others might be asked to do, or *get* to do, or to experience, is important counsel for modern disciples as well. We should quit measuring what the Lord gives to us by comparing our circumstances to others. Such behavior is almost always motivated by pride. C. S. Lewis reminds us: "Pride gets no pleasure out of having something, only out of having more of it than the next man. . . . It is the comparison that makes you proud: the pleasure of being above the rest. Once the element of competition has gone, pride has gone" (*Mere Christianity,* 110).

From information not known through any biblical texts but revealed only to the Prophet Joseph Smith, we learn that Jesus had earlier spoken to the apostle John about what he most desired in the future. And the beloved disciple asked to have power over death so he could remain on earth until the second coming of Christ in glory and bring souls unto him. It was on account of this previous arrangement that Peter asked the Lord about John's future activities (D&C 7:1–8).

John was granted his desire, and he became a translated being, like the Three Nephites. Of those individuals Elder McConkie stated:

> A change is wrought in their bodies so they cannot die at this time, but when the Lord comes again they "shall be changed in the twinkling of an eye from mortality to immortality," and thus they "shall never taste of death" (3 Nephi 28:1–10, 36–40). They will be like a person who lives during the millennium. Of such the revelation says: "It is appointed to him to die at the age of man. Wherefore, children shall grow up until they become old; old men shall die; but they shall not sleep in the dust, but they shall be changed in the twinkling of an

eye" (D&C 63:50–51). Thus they shall die, in the sense indicated, but they shall not taste of death. (*Doctrinal New Testament Commentary*, 1:865).

Interestingly, the Prophet Joseph Smith said, "John the Revelator [is] among the ten tribes of Israel who had been led away by Shalmaneser, king of Assyria, to prepare them for their return from their long dispersion, to again possess the land of their fathers" (Jackson, *Joseph Smith's Commentary on the Bible*, 142).

A Mountain in Galilee

After Jesus appeared to seven of his apostles at the Sea of Tiberias, all eleven surviving members of the Quorum of the Twelve met together and went "into a mountain where Jesus had appointed them" (Matthew 28:16). There the Savior met with these brethren and gave them important instructions regarding their divine commission to lead the kingdom after he was gone.

Apparently, other disciples were also present at the pre-appointed mountain conference because Matthew records that "they worshipped him: but some doubted" (Matthew 28:17). Surely the doubters were not the apostles but others who had not yet seen their Master and did not yet comprehend the literal physical, bodily nature of his resurrection. Elder McConkie writes that this "is likely the occasion of which, as Paul wrote later, 'he was seen of above five hundred brethren at once' (1 Cor. 15:6). If so, the seventies and leading brethren of the Church would have been present, as also perhaps the faithful women who are inheritors of like rewards with obedient priesthood holders" (*Doctrinal New Testament Commentary*, 1:866).

To his special witnesses, Jesus explained the all-encompassing authority and power he possessed but was now delegating to

179

them and expecting them to uphold: "All power is given unto me in heaven and in earth," he said. "Go ye therefore, and teach all nations, baptizing them in the name of the Father, and of the Son, and of the Holy Ghost: Teaching them to observe all things whatsoever I have commanded you: and, lo, I am with you alway, even unto the end of the world. Amen" (Matthew 28:18–20). The Gospel of Mark reports that Jesus also spoke to the apostles about the powerful and distinctive signs that would follow or attend all of those who believed on his name and were baptized: "In my name shall they cast out devils; they shall speak with new tongues; they shall take up serpents; and if they drink any deadly thing, it shall not hurt them: they shall lay hands on the sick, and they shall recover" (Mark 16:17–18). These remarkable promises were realized by many later on, as the book of Acts indicates.

The instructions that the Savior gave to his apostles on the mountain in Galilee serve to reinforce to modern disciples the mission and message of the Lord's true Church in every age. Those instructions clarify and emphasize that *the apostles are the Church's foundation*. They hold the keys in every age or dispensation when the Lord's Church is on the earth. All things in the Lord's Church—power, authority, general instructions, ordinances, and the like—come from Jesus Christ through his authorized representatives, the apostles. Regarding this last dispensation, President Brigham Young summarized the role of apostles when he said: "The keys of the eternal Priesthood, which is after the order of the Son of God, are comprehended by being an apostle. All the Priesthood, all the keys, all the gifts, all the endowments, and everything preparatory to entering into the presence of the Father and of the Son, are in, composed of, circumscribed by, or I might say incorporated within the circumference of, the Apostleship" (*Journal of Discourses*, 1:134–35).

With the convening of this mountain conference in Galilee, the Savior had now given the great missionary charge to his earthly leaders. By this point he had appeared several times to his apostles and disciples to confirm his living reality. This was the essence of his forty-day ministry. The foundation was firmly in place. Many came to know that the resurrection is real, and this gave them the strength to live the gospel of Jesus Christ and preach it to others. Because the ancient disciples knew with certainty that Jesus was the Christ, that he had in reality come back to life, that the promises of resurrection and eternal life were unequivocally true, they could face anything—and many did.

This conviction of the reality of the resurrection is alive and well in our day; it is the linchpin of our faith. With glad hearts Latter-day Saints proclaim the good news: Jesus is alive today and resides in yonder heavens with his divine Father, who is also a glorified man of flesh and bone and who has promised each of us that we can join them and be like them if we commit our lives to them. It is up to us.

And there are also many other things which Jesus did, the which, if they should be written every one, I suppose that even the world itself could not contain the books that should be written. Amen.

JOHN 21:25

And when he had spoken these things, while they beheld, he was taken up; and a cloud received him out of their sight.

And while they looked stedfastly toward heaven as he went up, behold, two men stood by them in white apparel;

Which also said, Ye men of Galilee, why stand ye gazing up into heaven? this same Jesus, which is taken up from you into heaven, shall so come in like manner as ye have seen him go into heaven.

ACTS 1:9–11

CHAPTER 8

Concluding His Earthly Ministry

We do not know a great deal about the rest of the Savior's postresurrection ministry among his disciples in the Holy Land, but from clues in biblical and non-biblical texts, we understand that other instruction he gave during his forty-day ministry had a temple orientation.

In the concluding verses of Luke's Gospel, which report Jesus' last instructions to the disciples just before his ascension, we read:

> And, behold, I send the promise of my Father upon you: but tarry ye in the city of Jerusalem, until ye be endued with power from on high.
>
> And he led them out as far as to Bethany, and he lifted up his hands, and blessed them.
>
> And it came to pass, while he blessed them, he was parted from them, and carried up into heaven.
>
> And they worshipped him, and returned to Jerusalem with great joy:
>
> And were continually in the temple, praising and blessing God. Amen. (Luke 24:49–53)

I do not think it coincidental that Luke reports that Jesus told his disciple-leaders to wait in Jerusalem until they "be endued with power from on high," and then Luke concludes his record by telling us emphatically that they were "continually in the temple" (Luke 24:49, 53). Of these verses, Elder Bruce R. McConkie wrote:

> It is common in Christendom to suppose that Jesus here commanded his apostles to tarry in Jerusalem until the promised gift of the Holy Ghost was received, which gift would constitute an endowment of power from on high. Perhaps the statement can be so used, for certainly the disciples were marvelously and powerfully endowed when the Holy Spirit came into their lives on the day of Pentecost (Acts 2).
>
> But from latter-day revelation we learn that the Lord had something more in mind in issuing this instruction. In this dispensation, after the elders had received the gift of the Holy Ghost and as early as January, 1831, the Lord began to reveal unto them that he had an endowment in store for the faithful (D&C 38:22; 43:16), "a blessing such as is not known among the children of men" (D&C 39:15). In June, 1833, he said: "I gave unto you a commandment that you should build a house, in the which house I design to endow those whom I have chosen with power from on high; For this is the promise of the Father unto you; therefore I command you to tarry, even as mine apostles at Jerusalem" (D&C 95:8–9; 105:11–12, 18, 33).
>
> Thus the apostles—or any ministers or missionaries in any age—are not fully qualified to go forth, preach the

gospel, and build up the kingdom, unless they have the gift of the Holy Ghost and also are endowed with power from on high, meaning have received certain knowledge, powers, and special blessings, normally given only in the Lord's Temple. (*Doctrinal New Testament Commentary,* 1:859)

Even more impressive than the way Luke concludes his Gospel is the way he begins his sequel, the Acts of the Apostles:

The former treatise have I made, O Theophilus, of all that Jesus began both to do and teach.

Until the day in which he was taken up, after that he through the Holy Ghost had given commandments unto the apostles whom he had chosen:

To whom also he shewed himself alive after his *passion* by many *infallible proofs,* being seen of them forty days, and speaking of the things pertaining to the kingdom of God. (Acts 1:1–3; emphasis added)

The word *passion* in this text derives from the Latin *passus* and means "sufferings," as the Joseph Smith Translation also denotes. The phrase "infallible proofs" is much more vivid in the original Greek from which the English is translated. The Greek word here, *tekmeriois,* means "sure signs or tokens" (*Greek-English Lexicon,* 695). In other words, Jesus instructed his disciples during his forty-day ministry using many "sure signs or tokens" and spoke of things pertaining to the kingdom of God. Indeed! The Prophet Joseph Smith taught that in order to obtain eternal life all individuals, no matter the dispensation in which they lived, must follow the same plan of salvation, obey the same principles and ordinances, that were instituted *before* the world was created, and full salvation cannot be obtained without these ordinances. Furthermore, the only place where these ordinances can be obtained is in the house of the Lord, or a like place designated by the Lord when, for example, a temple has not yet been constructed.

This important doctrine is found in many of the Prophet Joseph Smith's sermons and was summarized very powerfully in a discourse given in June 1843. At that time the Prophet declared:

> It was the design of the councils of heaven before the world was, that the principles and laws of the priesthood should be predicated upon the gathering of the people in every age of the world. Jesus did everything to gather the people, and they would not be gathered. . . . Ordinances instituted in the heavens before the foundation of the world, in the priesthood, for the salvation of men, are not to be altered or changed. All must be saved on the same principles.
>
> It is for the same purpose that God gathers together His people in the last days, to build unto the Lord a house to prepare them for the ordinances and endowments, washings and anointings, etc. (*History of the Church*, 5:423–24)

And then the Prophet made this significant comment:

> If a man gets a fullness of the priesthood of God, he has to get it in the same way that Jesus Christ obtained it, and that was by keeping all the commandments and obeying all the ordinances of the house of the Lord. . . .
>
> All men who become heirs of God and joint-heirs with Jesus Christ will have to receive the fulness of the

ordinances of his kingdom; and those who will not receive all the ordinances will come short of the fullness of that glory, if they do not lose the whole. (*History of the Church*, 5:424)

It becomes clear to us from nonbiblical sources that the ordinances of exaltation were available to the Lord's disciples in the meridian of time. President Heber C. Kimball taught that the temple endowment available to us in our present dispensation is the same, in principle, as was available in the ancient Church of Jesus Christ. He also said that Jesus "was the one that inducted his Apostles into these ordinances" (*Journal of Discourses*, 10:241). President Joseph Fielding Smith and Elder Bruce R. McConkie stated their belief that Peter, James, and John received the endowment on the Mount of Transfiguration (*Doctrines of Salvation*, 2:165, 170; *Doctrinal New Testament Commentary*, 1:400). Because the chief apostles were commanded by the Savior not to discuss what happened on the Mount of Transfiguration until after Jesus was "risen again from the dead" (Matthew 17:9), it is thought by some gospel scholars that temple ordinances were not administered to the rest of the Twelve, or other worthy members of the Church, until *after* the resurrection of Jesus Christ (Pace, "What It Means to Know Christ," 51).

This view is supported both by certain apocryphal texts that describe Jesus' forty-day postresurrection ministry as a time when our Lord taught the mysteries of the kingdom and established a sacred ritual among his disciples and also by writings that detail the history of the ancient Church. The fourth-century historian Eusebius of Caesarea (260–340) included this stunning statement in his work entitled *Ecclesiastical History:* "After the resurrection, the Lord imparted the higher knowledge to James the Just, John, and Peter. They gave it to the other apostles, and the other apostles to the Seventy" (Maier, *Eusebius*, 58).

Of all the texts in the New Testament itself, the writings of the apostle John are the most transparent in divulging temple teachings and connections, which Jesus taught to the eleven apostles as well as other disciples during his forty-day ministry. John alone speaks of the following:

1. The ordinance of the washing of the feet (John 13)

2. The Second Comforter (John 14)

3. Becoming kings and priests (Revelation 1)

4. The crown of life (Revelation 2)

5. A white stone and a new name (Revelation 2)

6. Power over the nations (Revelation 2)

7. White raiment and the book of life (Revelation 3)

8. Becoming a pillar in God's temple (Revelation 3)

9. Being granted the privilege of sitting with the Lord in his throne (Revelation 4)

We usually say that John wrote for members of the Church of Jesus Christ. It would, perhaps, be more accurate to say that he wrote for members of Christ's Church who knew about the principles and ordinances of the temple and the endowments of knowledge and power received in them.

It should not surprise us that so many independent sources, both those within the Church and those outside it, link the instruction Jesus gave to his disciples after his resurrection with the temple, higher knowledge, and endowments of power.

Resurrection and the temple go together. In the temple the priest-hood ordinance of resurrection is prefigured; we are presented with a pattern of how the resurrection will occur. In the temple we are taught the reasons that resurrection is so important. In the temple we are taught the destiny of resurrected beings. In the temple we are given the covenants and powers that exalted resur-rected beings will use. In the temple we are taught the same con-cepts that the Messiah, the first to be resurrected, taught to his followers anciently. The temple is the home of resurrected beings, specifically the Lord himself. The temple is literally his earthly house. It is truly exciting to belong to the Lord's Church and to see how consistent it has been in its operation and teachings from dispensation to dispensation.

THE DOCTRINE OF RESURRECTION ACCORDING TO PAUL

In addition to instructing his disciples regarding the myster-ies of the kingdom, the scriptures tell us that Jesus made other appearances to individuals and groups both before and after his ascension. He confirmed the reality of his bodily resurrection and showed to those he visited what resurrected bodies are like. One of those Jesus visited and instructed was the apostle Paul (1 Corinthians 15:8), who, in turn, helped others understand the doctrine of resurrection by discussing it in one of his major epistles (1 Corinthians 15). Paul began his discussion by listing many of those to whom the Savior appeared before his ascen-sion. Notable among these was James, the half-brother of Jesus. James did not believe that his half-brother was the Messiah while Jesus lived among them before his crucifixion (Matthew 13:55; John 7:1–5). But after the Resurrection, James was found among the community of believers (Acts 1:14) and even became a stal-wart in the Jerusalem branch of the Church (Acts 15:13).

Though we do not know exactly when or where Jesus appeared to his half-brother, we believe it was the likely turning point in James's life, the time when he came to know that his half-brother, Jesus, really was who he said he was all along. It is heartwarming to think of Jesus taking special spiritual care of the members of his own family, ministering to them and nurturing their faith after they had endured what must have been very challenging circumstances. I think it could not have been easy for even fundamentally good people to live in the shadow of Jesus in a family setting, to witness his exceptional life, to watch his perfect behavior, and to experience his unique perceptions of the world without developing both positive and negative feel-ings. In addition, as Jesus grew older he undoubtedly began to draw ridicule and persecution. This would have affected the family. Jesus blessed his half-brother's life eternally by visiting him as the resurrected Messiah, and we appreciate Paul's note about this.

Paul's unparalleled contribution to our understanding of the resurrection is to be found in his comprehensive explanation of it in 1 Corinthians 15. Paul certifies that Jesus was the first to be resurrected, making it possible for all to follow (1 Corinthians 15:15–16, 20). Paul also explains that resurrection itself is redemption, for "if Christ be not raised . . . ye are yet in your sins" (1 Corinthians 15:17). This is so, as the Book of Mormon explains, because without the resurrection our spirits after phys-ical death would increasingly come under the influence and con-trol of Satan who is a spirit, until, without the regeneration that resurrection brings, we would "become like unto him, and we become devils, angels to a devil, to be shut out from the presence of our God" (2 Nephi 9:9). Hence, as Joseph Smith knew, "the resurrection from the dead is the redemption of the soul" (D&C 88:16). The resurrection works in tandem with Christ's infinite and incomprehensible suffering to redeem and rescue us from the lasting effects of sin. These different aspects of the Atonement fit together in perfect, cohesive harmony.

Paul also knew and taught that the resurrection is so powerful and all-encompassing in its redemptive effects that it overcomes and makes right *all* the negative effects of the fall of Adam: "As in Adam all die [physically and spiritually], even so in Christ shall all be made alive [physically and spiritually]" (1 Corinthians 15:22). That is, the resurrection overcomes physical death by giving us immortal physical bodies; it overcomes spiritual death by bringing *every* soul back into the presence of the Lord to be judged, even if only for a short period. Whether or not we will remain in the presence of the Lord is determined by what our own actions were in mortality. But Christ's resurrection, which makes possible our own resurrection, overcomes the spiritual effects of Adam's transgression, which transmitted spiritual death (separation from God) to all the posterity of Adam and Eve—all of us! Thus, the resurrection is inextricably tied to the Fall. President Ezra Taft Benson said:

> The plan of redemption must start with the account of the fall of Adam. In the words of Moroni, "By Adam came the fall of man. And because of the fall of man came Jesus Christ. . . . and because of Jesus Christ came the redemption of man" (Mormon 9:12).
>
> Just as man does not really desire food until he is hungry, so he does not desire the salvation of Christ until he knows why he needs Christ.

No one adequately and properly knows why he needs Christ until he understands and accepts the doctrine of the Fall and its effect upon all mankind. (Conference Report, April 1987, 106)

I make a point of this principle because as a new missionary years ago, I used to teach the doctrine incorrectly by saying that only those who kept the commandments would overcome the effects of spiritual death and that only the righteous would be brought back into the presence of the Lord. Perhaps this came about through a misreading of Alma 11:41: "The wicked remain as though there had been no redemption made, except it be the loosing of the bands of death." The great prophet, Samuel the Lamanite, set me straight. Spiritual death is overcome for all; however, whether or not an individual will suffer a second spiritual death depends upon that individual's repentance and the fruits that flow from it:

> For behold, he [Christ] surely must die that salvation may come; yea, it behooveth him and becometh expedient that he dieth, to bring to pass the resurrection of the dead, that thereby men may be brought into the presence of the Lord.

> Yea, behold, this death bringeth to pass the resurrection, and redeemeth all mankind from the first death— that spiritual death; for all mankind, by the fall of Adam being cut off from the presence of the Lord, are considered as dead, both as to things temporal and to things spiritual.

> But behold, the resurrection of Christ redeemeth mankind, yea, even all mankind, and bringeth them back into the presence of the Lord.

Yea, and it bringeth to pass the condition of repentance, that whosoever repenteth the same is not hewn down and cast into the fire; but whosoever repenteth not is hewn down and cast into the fire; and there cometh upon them again a spiritual death, yea, a second death, for they are cut off again as to things pertaining to righteousness.

Therefore repent ye, repent ye, lest by knowing these things and not doing them ye shall suffer yourselves to come under condemnation, and ye are brought down unto this second death. (Helaman 14:15–19)

Another important aspect that comes out of Paul's discussion concerns the different times and degrees of the resurrection. Our Heavenly Father's sons and daughters are not all resurrected at the same time. Every individual is made alive "in his own order: Christ the firstfruits; afterward they that are Christ's at his coming" (1 Corinthians 15:23).

In the resurrection, celestial bodies will come forth first, in the "morning" of the first resurrection. Their graves will be opened, and they will be caught up to meet the Savior at his second coming. They will descend with him to rule and reign as kings and queens. Those with terrestrial bodies will come forth next, in the "afternoon" of the first resurrection, after the Savior has ushered in the Millennium. At the end of the Millennium, those with telestial bodies will begin to come forth. The last to be resurrected will be those possessing bodies fit for no kingdom of glory—sons of perdition (McConkie, *Mormon Doctrine*, 640; JST 1 Corinthians 15:40–42).

Each of these kinds of resurrected bodies possesses a different glory, power, and potential. Those raised with celestial bodies overcome all things and dwell with God and Christ forever. They can become like God. But those not raised with celestial bodies cannot dwell with God and Christ, cannot become exactly like them, "worlds without end" (D&C 76:112; see also vv. 50–62). As the Prophet Joseph Smith explained, "In the resurrection, some are raised to be angels, others are raised to become Gods" (*Teachings of the Prophet Joseph Smith*, 312).

Thus, at the time of resurrection there is a judgment and separation, just as there is at the time of physical death. (The righteous go to paradise; the unrighteous, to prison.) This is not the final judgment but preparatory to it. There will be no surprises at the time of the final judgment. Individuals will already possess immortal bodies of varying powers and capabilities, which determine their destiny for eternity. Judgment and resurrection are linked together. Resurrection does not occur without the rendering of a verdict. Elder McConkie stated:

> It is very evident that men will not have to await the day of final judgment—the formal occasion when every living soul will stand before the judgment bar, an event that will not take place until the last soul has been resurrected—to learn their status and the degree of glory they are to receive in eternity. Those who are living a telestial law will be swept off the earth at the Second Coming. (D&C 101:24; Mal. 3:4.) Those who come forth in the morning of the first resurrection, who "are Christ's, the firstfruits," will have celestial bodies and go to a celestial kingdom. "Those who are Christ's at his coming" will come forth with terrestrial bodies and go to a terrestrial kingdom. Similarly those coming forth in the beginning of the second resurrection will have telestial

bodies and go to a telestial kingdom, while the sons of perdition, the last to be resurrected, will have bodies capable of receiving no glory and will be cast out with the devil and his angels forever (D&C 88:98–102).

No one has yet been resurrected with any kind of a body except a celestial. Those who were with Christ in his resurrection will all have eternal inheritance in his celestial presence (D&C 133:54–56). Though there is yet to be a day of formal judgment for all men, yet there is no question, for instance, of the reward that Abraham, Isaac, and Jacob will receive in that day. "They have entered into their exaltation, according to the promises, and sit upon thrones, and are not angels but are gods," the revelation records. (D&C 132:29–37.) The same is true of Adam, Enoch, Noah, Moses, and the faithful saints from the beginning to the day of Christ. (*Mormon Doctrine*, 404)

THE RESTORATION OF THE EARTH

Truly, resurrection is part of the great law of restoration. The law of restoration dictates that all things created by our Father in Heaven or by Jesus Christ (under his Father's direction) will be redeemed and restored by Jesus Christ—all things! Restoration *is* the redemptive work of Christ. The earth and every living thing on it will be restored to its proper and perfect frame. For mortals, not even a hair of our heads will be lost in the resurrection (Alma 40:23).

What Adam's fall took away, Jesus' atonement restores. All things will be renewed. Even this earth will be restored to its original, created position in the presence of God (Abraham 5:13). When Adam fell, this earth also fell and took up its present position. Resurrection will rectify this aspect of the Fall. President Joseph Fielding Smith said: "When this earth was created, it was not according to our present time, but it was created according to Kolob's time, for the Lord has said it was created on celestial time which is Kolob's time. Then he revealed to Abraham that Adam was subject to Kolob's time before his transgression" (*Doctrines of Salvation*, 1:79).

President Brigham Young presents an even clearer picture of the destiny of this earth owing to Christ's atonement and resurrection:

> When the earth was framed and brought into existence and man was placed upon it, it was near the throne of our Father in heaven. . . . but when man fell, the earth feel into space, and took up its abode in this planetary system, and the sun became our light. When the Lord said—"Let there be light," there was light, for the earth was brought near the sun that it might reflect upon it so as to give us light by day, and the moon to give us light by night. This is the glory the earth came from, and when it is glorified it will return again unto the presence of the Father, and it will dwell there, and these intelligent beings that I am looking at, if they live worthy of it, will dwell upon this earth. (*Journal of Discourses*, 17:143)

THE ASCENSION

Having finished the work of his forty-day ministry, the Savior was ready to bid farewell to his beloved associates, the apostles. He led them as far as Bethany, on the eastern slope of the Mount of Olives, and gave them final instructions.

Luke records that Jesus commanded the apostles to remain

in Jerusalem until the promised arrival of and immersion in the powers of the Holy Ghost were realized (Acts 1:4–5). The brethren then queried the Lord about the restoration of the great religious and political kingdom that will attend the second coming and millennial reign of Christ on earth, just as the pre-meridian prophets foresaw. Was it to happen during their life-time? Jesus told them that it was not for them to know the exact timing of these events. They needed to be patient and pursue their commission as special witnesses of the Resurrection, start-ing in Jerusalem and Judea and spreading out to the uttermost parts of the earth (Acts 1:8).

As the apostles contemplated these instructions, as well as their future, Jesus ascended in a cloud of glory and was gone. But two angelic witnesses appeared and provided important com-mentary on this experience, which is also for all disciples of this dispensation. Jesus' ascension is a model for his glorious second coming. He will descend from his heavenly throne to appear on the Mount of Olives and reign on the earth as King of Israel, King of Kings. Thus, Jesus' ascension brings us back full circle to the beginning of his atoning experience, forty-three days earlier, and propels us forward to the start of a new era. "The Mount of Olives, 'the olive-orchard'—hallowed spot! On this Mount is the Garden called Gethsemane where Jesus in agony took upon himself the sins of the world . . . here he now ascends in triumphant glory; and here he shall return in that same glory to begin his reign as Israel's King. (D. & C. 133:19–20.)" (McConkie, *Doctrinal New Testament Commentary*, 2:28).

SPECIAL WITNESSES

After witnessing their Master's ascension from Olivet and thus fulfilling another aspect of their role as special witnesses, the apostles returned to Jerusalem to await the coming of the Comforter in power and then begin teaching the world the gospel of the living God. The core of this gospel message was and is and forever will be the atonement and resurrection of Jesus Christ. The apostles, as well as the other disciples in the meridian dispensation, now knew with eyewitness-certainty that Jesus had risen from the grave and opened a way for all to follow. So impressive are the number of encounters with the risen Lord, and so credible the documentation of these episodes, that one non-Latter-day Saint expert on the New Testament stated categorically:

> The evidence for the resurrection of Jesus Christ is overwhelming. Nothing in history is more certain than that the disciples believed that, after being crucified, dead, and buried, Christ rose again from the tomb on the third day, and that at intervals thereafter he met and conversed with them. The most obvious proof that they believed this is the existence of the Christian church. . . .
>
> It is a commonplace that every event in history must have an adequate cause. Never were hopes more desolate than when Jesus of Nazareth was taken down from the cross and laid in the tomb. Stricken with grief at the death of their Master, the disciples were dazed and bewildered. Their mood was one of dejection and defeat, reflected in the spiritless words of the Emmaus travelers, "We had hoped that he was the one to redeem Israel" (Luke 24:21). A short time later the same group of disciples was aglow with supreme confidence and fearless in the face of persecution. Their message was one of joy and

triumph. What caused such a radical change in these men's lives? The explanation is that something unprecedented had occurred: Jesus Christ was raised from the dead! Fifty-some days after the crucifixion the apostolic preaching of Christ's resurrection began in Jerusalem with such power and persuasion that the evidence convinced thousands. (Metzger, *New Testament*, 126–27)

We may summarize the impressive list of witnesses to the Lord's resurrection (witnesses as well to the empty Garden Tomb) as they have been recorded in scripture. These are arranged in approximate chronological order, as nearly as we can tell.

1. Mary Magdalene (John 20:1–18), outside the Garden Tomb on the morning of Jesus' resurrection

2. Other women (Matthew 28:1–9), somewhere between the Garden Tomb and Jerusalem on Resurrection morning

3. Cleopas and another disciple (Mark 16:12–13; Luke 24:13–32), on the road to Emmaus on Resurrection day

4. Simon Peter (Luke 24:34; 1 Corinthians 15:5), on Resurrection day

5. Ten of the Twelve (Luke 24:36–53; John 20:19–24), in a closed room somewhere in Jerusalem on Resurrection night

6. Eleven of the Twelve (Mark 16:14; John 20:26–31), in a closed room in Jerusalem one week after the Resurrection

7. Seven of the Twelve (John 21:1–14), at the Sea of Galilee (Tiberias), the third visit to the group

8. Eleven of the Twelve (Matthew 28:16–20), on a mountain in Galilee by previous appointment of the Savior

9. More than five hundred brethren at once (1 Corinthians 15:6), probably on the mountain in Galilee with the eleven apostles

10. James (1 Corinthians 15:7)

11. Eleven apostles at Jesus' ascension (Mark 16:14, 19; Luke 24: 50–51; Acts 1:3–11), near Bethany forty days after the Resurrection

12. Saul of Tarsus (1 Corinthians 9:1; 15:8), on the road to Damascus, Syria

13. The Nephites (3 Nephi 11:1–18:39; 19:2, 15–26:15), in the land Bountiful in America near the temple about A.D. 34

14. John the Revelator (Revelation 1:9–18), on the Isle of Patmos sometime between 81 A.D. and 96

15. The Nephite Twelve (3 Nephi 27:1–28:12)

16. Lost tribes of Israel (3 Nephi 16:1–4; 17:4), soon after the Savior's visitation to the Nephite people

17. Mormon (Mormon 1:15)

18. Moroni (Ether 12:39)

19. Joseph Smith (Joseph Smith–History 1:14–20), in the Sacred Grove near Palmyra, New York, in the spring of 1820

Many of these witnesses were visited by the resurrected Lord more than once. But it does not end there. The chain of witnesses to the Lord's resurrection and living reality continues. Many are the accounts and testimonies that tell of individuals since 1820 who have come to *know* that Jesus of Nazareth lives as a resurrected Being. One of the better-known accounts of the resurrected Lord appearing in these latter days comes from Allie Young Pond, granddaughter of Church president Lorenzo Snow. She related this episode:

> One evening while I was visiting Grandpa Snow in his room in the Salt Lake Temple, I remained until the door keepers had gone and the night-watchmen had not yet come in, so grandpa said he would take me to the main front entrance and let me out that way. He got this bunch of keys from his dresser. After we left his room, and while we were still in the large corridor leading into the celestial room, I was walking several steps ahead of grandpa when he stopped me and said: "Wait a moment, Allie, I want to tell you something. It was right here that the Lord Jesus Christ appeared to me at the time of the death of President Woodruff. He instructed me to go right ahead and reorganize the First Presidency of the Church at once and not wait as had been done after the death of the previous presidents, and that I was to succeed President Woodruff."
>
> Then grandpa came a step nearer and held out his left hand and said: "He stood right here, about three feet above the floor. It looked as though He stood on a plate of solid gold."
>
> Grandpa told me what a glorious personage the Savior is and described His hands, feet, countenance and beautiful white robes, all of which were of such a glory of whiteness and brightness that he could hardly gaze upon Him.

Then he came another step nearer and put his right hand on my head and said: "Now granddaughter, I want you to remember that this is the testimony of your grandfather, that he told you with his own lips that he actually saw the Savior, here in the Temple, and talked with him face to face. (*Best-Loved Stories of the LDS People*, 239–40)

Closer to our day, President Harold B. Lee, eleventh president of The Church of Jesus Christ of Latter-day Saints, presented his powerful and thought-provoking witness:

Some years ago two missionaries came to me with what seemed to them to be a very difficult question. A young . . . minister had laughed at them when they had said that Apostles were necessary today in order for the true Church to be upon the earth. They said that the minister said, "Do you realize that when the Apostles met to choose one to fill the vacancy caused by the death of Judas, they said it had to be one who companied with them and had been a witness of all things pertaining to the mission and resurrection of the Lord? How can you say you have Apostles, if that be the measure of an Apostle?"

And so these young men said, "What shall we answer?"

I said to them, "Go back and ask your minister friend two questions. First, how did the Apostle Paul gain what was necessary to be called an Apostle? He didn't know the Lord, had no personal acquaintance. He hadn't accompanied the Apostles. He hadn't been a witness of the ministry nor of the resurrection of the Lord. How did he gain his testimony sufficient to be an Apostle? And the second question you ask him is, How does he know that all who are today Apostles have not likewise received that witness?"

I bear witness to you that those who hold the apostolic calling may, and do, know of the reality of the mission of the Lord. (*Teachings of Harold B. Lee,* 546–47)

And finally, President Ezra Taft Benson, twelfth president of The Church of Jesus Christ of Latter-day Saints, offered this testimony that serves as a fitting summary of all such witnesses:

Since the day of resurrection when Jesus became the "firstfruits of them that slept," there have been those who disbelieve and scoff. They maintain there is no life beyond mortal existence. Some have even written books which contain their fanciful heresies to suggest how Jesus' disciples perpetrated the hoax of His resurrection.

But I say unto you, the resurrection of Jesus Christ is the greatest historical event in the world to date.

In this dispensation, commencing with the Prophet Joseph Smith, the witnesses are legion. As one of those called as special witnesses, I add my testimony to those fellow Apostles: He lives! He lives with resurrected body. There is no truth or fact of which I am more assured, or *know better by personal experience,* than the truth of the literal resurrection of our Lord. ("Five Marks of the Divinity of Jesus Christ," 48; emphasis added)

God be thanked for such witnesses as these in our own day.

FINAL THOUGHTS

The story of the Garden Tomb is the culmination of the story of Gethsemane and the story of Golgotha. Its effect is powerful and unforgettable. It describes the foundation of our future. It is a story for all humanity.

For every soul who carries a burden, for every soul who faces a challenge, for every soul who harbors a heartache, for every soul who perseveres through pain, for every soul who is plagued by fears, for every soul who seeks comfort, for every soul who has faced death, for every soul who has lost a loved one, for every soul who has seen horror, for every soul—the message of the Garden Tomb is intended. The message is this: the tomb is empty; Jesus is alive today; he is the literal Son of God, our Heavenly Father; he was resurrected; he alone made it possible and inevitable for every human being who has ever lived to live again; he has guaranteed that we will see our loved ones again; he has all power; he paid for every sin; he knows all suffering; he knows the name of each one of us; he and his Father hear our every prayer. If the Atonement is not for everyone, it will not be for anyone! All Creation is affected by the resurrection of Jesus Christ.

When all is said and done, there has never been nor ever will be anything so powerful, so majestic, so wondrous, so merciful as the atonement of Jesus Christ. There are no words capable of describing the infinite goodness and omnipotence of Jesus. As the apostle John testified, the time is coming for the followers of the Lord when "God shall wipe away all tears from their eyes; and there shall be no more death, neither sorrow, nor crying, neither shall there be any more pain: for the former things are passed away" (Revelation 21:4). The power by which all this is accomplished is the infinite atonement of Jesus Christ. The grace he extends to us is freely given, but it did not come free. Its cost was infinite, and yet he asks no price. All that he wants from us is our loyalty and love and gratitude.

God be thanked for his matchless gift.

Sources

Allen, James B. *Trials of Discipleship: The Story of William Clayton, a Mormon.* Urbana: University of Illinois Press, 1987.

Andrus, Hyrum L. *God, Man, and the Universe.* Salt Lake City: Deseret Book, 1968.

Benson, Ezra Taft. "Five Marks of the Divinity of Jesus Christ." Address to Latter-day Saint Student Association (LDSSA) fireside, University of Utah, Salt Lake City, 9 December 1979.

———. "Civic Standards for the Faithful Saints." *Ensign*, July 1972.

———. *The Teachings of Ezra Taft Benson.* Salt Lake City: Bookcraft, 1988.

Best-Loved Stories of the LDS People. Edited by Jack M. Lyon et al. Salt Lake City: Deseret Book, 1992.

Cannon, George Q. *Gospel Truth.* 2 vols. in 1. Edited by Jerreld L. Newquist. Salt Lake City: Deseret Book, 1987.

Chadwick, Jeffrey R. "Revisiting Golgotha and the Garden Tomb." *Religious Educator* 4, no. 1 (2003): 16.

Collected Discourses of the First Presidency and the Twelve. Edited by Brian H. Stuy. 5 vols. Sandy, Utah: B.H.S. Publishing, 1992.

Conference Report. Salt Lake City: The Church of Jesus Christ of Latter-day Saints, 1966–87.

Ehat, Andrew F., and Lyndon W. Cook., eds. *The Words of Joseph Smith.* Orem, Utah: Grandin Book, 1991.

Eusebius. *The Ecclesiastical History*. Vol. 1. Translated by Kirsopp Lake. Cambridge, Mass.: Harvard University Press, 1992.

Farrar, Frederic W. *The Life of Christ*. New York: Cassell, 1902.

Hinckley, Bryant S. *Sermons and Missionary Services of Melvin Joseph Ballard*. Salt Lake City: Deseret Book, 1949.

Hunter, Howard W. Conference Report, April 1986.

Holland, Jeffrey R. *"Therefore, What?"* Address delivered at Brigham Young University, Provo, Utah, 8 August 2000.

The Interpreter's Bible. 12 vols. Nashville: Abingdon, 1951.

Jackson, Kent P. *Joseph Smith's Commentary on the Bible*. Salt Lake City: Deseret Book, 1994.

Josephus, Flavius. *Josephus: Complete Works*. Translated by William Whiston. Grand Rapids, Mich.: Kregel Publications, 1960.

Journal of Discourses. 26 vols. London: Latter-day Saints' Book Depot, 1854–86.

Keller, W. Phillip. *Rabboni, Which Is to Say, Master*. Grand Rapids, Mich.: Kregel Publications, 1997.

Kimball, Spencer W. "Visit Leads Prophet to Walk in Holy Places." *Church News*, 3 November 1979, 4.

Kloner, Amos. "Did a Rolling Stone Close Jesus' Tomb?" *Biblical Archaeology Review*, September/October 1999, 23.

Lee, Harold B. "I Walked Today Where Jesus Walked." *Ensign*, April 1972, 3.

———. "Qualities of Leadership." Address to Latter-day Saint Student Association (LDSSA) Convention, Salt Lake City, August 1970.

———. *The Teachings of Harold B. Lee*. Edited by Clyde J. Williams. Salt Lake City: Bookcraft, 1996.

A Lexicon, Abridged from Liddell and Scott's Greek-English Lexicon. Oxford: Clarendon Press, 1871.

Lewis, C. S. *Mere Christianity*. New York: Touchstone, 1980.

Littlefield, Lyman Omer. *Reminiscences of Latter-day Saints*. Logan, Utah: Utah Journal Co., 1888.

Mace, Wandle. "Journal of Wandle Mace." Typescript, Harold B. Lee Library, Brigham Young University, Provo, Utah.

Maier, Paul L. *Eusebius—The Church History: A New Translation with Commentary.* Grand Rapids, Mich.: Kregel Publications, 1999.

———. *In the Fullness of Time: A Historian Looks at Christmas, Easter, and the Early Church.* New York: HarperCollins Publishers, 1991.

Matthews, Victor H. *Manners and Customs of the Bible.* Rev. ed. Peabody, Mass.: Hendrickson Publishers, 1988, 1991.

Matthews, Robert J. "Resurrection: The Ultimate Triumph." In *Jesus Christ, Son of God, Savior.* Provo, Utah: Religious Studies Center, 2002.

McConkie, Bruce R. *Doctrinal New Testament Commentary.* 3 vols. Salt Lake City: Bookcraft, 1965–73.

———. *Mormon Doctrine.* 2d ed. Salt Lake City: Bookcraft, 1966.

———. *The Mortal Messiah.* 4 vols. Salt Lake City: Deseret Book, 1981.

———. "The Purifying Power of Gethsemane." *Ensign,* May 1985, 9.

———. "Probationary Test of Mortality." Address at Salt Lake Institute of Religion, Salt Lake City, Utah, 10 January 1982.

———. "The Salvation of Little Children." *Ensign,* April 1977, 3.

Metzger, Bruce Manning. *The New Testament: Its Background, Growth, and Content.* Nashville: Abingdon Press, 1965.

Millet, Robert L., and Joseph Fielding McConkie. *The Life Beyond.* Salt Lake City: Bookcraft, 1986.

Mumford, Thomas. *Horizontal Harmony of the Four Gospels in Parallel Columns.* Salt Lake City: Deseret Book, 1976.

Murphy-O'Connor, Jerome. "Fishers of Fish, Fishers of Men." *Bible Review,* June 1999, 23.

———. *The Holy Land: An Oxford Archaeological Guide from Earliest Times to 1700.* Oxford: Oxford University Press, 1998.

Nelson, Russell M. *From Heart to Heart: An Autobiography.* Salt Lake City, 1979.

Pace, George W. "What It Means to Know Christ." *Ensign,* September 1974.

Packer, Boyd K. "We Honor Now His Journey." *Ensign,* July 1994.

Pratt, Parley P. *Key to the Science of Theology.* Classics in Mormon Literature Series. Salt Lake City: Deseret Book, 1978.

SOURCES

Rousseau, John J., and Rami Arav. *Jesus and His World: An Archaeological and Cultural Dictionary.* Minneapolis: Augsburg Fortress, 1995.

Smith, Joseph. *Teachings of the Prophet Joseph Smith.* Selected by Joseph Fielding Smith. Salt Lake City: Deseret Book, 1976.

Smith, Joseph. *History of The Church of Jesus Christ of Latter-day Saints.* Edited by B. H. Roberts. 2d ed. rev. 7 vols. Salt Lake City: The Church of Jesus Christ of Latter-day Saints, 1932–51.

Smith, Joseph F. *Gospel Doctrine.* 5th ed. Salt Lake City: Deseret Book, 1966.

———. "The Resurrection." *Liahona—The Elders Journal* (8 August 1908): 178.

Smith, Joseph Fielding. *Answers to Gospel Questions.* Compiled by Joseph Fielding Smith, Jr. 5 vols. Salt Lake City: Deseret Book, 1957–66.

———. *Doctrines of Salvation.* Compiled by Bruce R. McConkie. 3 vols. Salt Lake City: Bookcraft, 1954–56.

———. "The First Presidency and the Council of the Twelve." *Improvement Era,* November 1966, 979.

Smith, Lucy Mack. *History of Joseph Smith by His Mother.* Edited by Preston Nibley. Salt Lake City: Bookcraft, 1954.

Special Witnesses of Christ [videotape]. Salt Lake City: The Church of Jesus Christ of Latter-day Saints, 2000.

Talmage, James E. *The Articles of Faith.* 12th ed. Salt Lake City: The Church of Jesus Christ of Latter-day Saints, 1924.

———. *Jesus the Christ.* 3d ed. Salt Lake City: Deseret Book, 1916.

Wachsman, Shelley. *The Sea of Galilee Boat: A 2000-Year-Old Discovery from the Sea of Legends.* Cambridge, Mass.: Perseus, 2000.

Walker, Peter. *The Weekend That Changed the World: The Mystery of Jerusalem's Empty Tomb.* Louisville, Ky.: Westminster John Knox Press, 2000.

Woodruff, Wilford. *The Discourses of Wilford Woodruff.* Selected and edited by G. Homer Durham. Salt Lake City: Bookcraft, 1969.

Young, Brigham. *Discourses of Brigham Young.* Selected by John A. Widtsoe. Salt Lake City: Deseret Book, 1971.

Index